THE OTHER AMERICA

THE OTHER AMERICA

by

Carl Stegmann

Rudolf Steiner College Press
Fair Oaks, California

This book appeared in German under the title, *Das Andere Amerika*, edited by Thomas Stöckli, published in 1991 by the Verlag am Goetheanum in Switzerland. It has been translated by Maria St. Goar.

Cover art by Julie Moyer

ISBN 0-945803-28-1

Printed in the United States of America.

Book orders may be made through
Rudolf Steiner College Bookstore
Tel. 916-961-8729, Fax 916-961-3032,
E-mail: bookstore@steinercollege.edu.

Rudolf Steiner College Press
9200 Fair Oaks Boulevard
Fair Oaks, CA 95628

CONTENTS

PART III: RALPH WALDO EMERSON - A HERALD OF THE FUTURE

REFLECTIONS ON EMERSON, GOETHE, AND RUDOLF STEINER

EMERSON, HELPER OF AMERICA'S FUTURE

APPENDIX

PREFACE TO THE
ENGLISH LANGUAGE EDITION

Now as we mark the 21st anniversary of the founding of Rudolf Steiner College, we are pleased to be able to offer my father's revised work, *The Other America,* in an English language edition. As we stand in the last years of this century, the recognition of the "inner, spiritual America" is an essential task not only for those of us who live in this country but also for those individuals around the world who look to America both in a critical and a supportive way.

Throughout his life, Carl Stegmann was a very active, will-oriented individual; he was a doer. The tasks he set for himself, he carried through with great energy and vitality. He found Anthroposophy at an early age through a book given to him by a friend. This book *How to Know Higher Worlds* became his "workbook," as he called it, for the rest of his life.

After having encountered this book, Carl had the immediate desire to meet Rudolf Steiner personally and to hear him speak. He had numerous occasions to do so; he even had the opportunity to see and experience the first Goetheanum in Switzerland. Meeting Rudolf Steiner and hearing him lecture inspired Carl throughout his life and filled him with strong impulses and a lasting inner enthusiasm for this modern path of knowledge, Anthroposophy.

Decisive for his whole life's work were the lectures Rudolf Steiner gave in Vienna at the West-East Congress in 1922. Carl was just 25, and his young wife Christine 20. It was possible for both of them to attend this conference by using a gift of money they had received to furnish their apartment. The thoughts that Rudolf Steiner expressed there would not only inspire Carl's immediate work but also bring him later in his life to North America. At this conference Rudolf Steiner presented his insights into the threefold structure of the world and the differences and true tasks of the East, the West and the Center. He also pointed to the similarity in the will-oriented approach to life of the working class of Europe and of the people in the West, the Americans.

The ideas that Rudolf Steiner presented there addressed deep inner questions that had lived in Carl's soul since he was a teenager. Having been raised in a working class milieu—his father was a worker in the ship-yards of the harbor in Kiel—he was exposed at a very early age to the concerns, issues, and aspirations of the workers. Many meetings took place in his father's home where he heard the workers debate the ideas of Kant, Marx and Lasalle. Carl had learned the locksmith's trade himself and therefore had firsthand experience of what the workers' world encompassed. Listening to Rudolf Steiner speak about the aspirations and talents of the working people, Carl Stegmann was convinced that Rudolf Steiner knew the workers better than anyone else.

After speaking to Dr. Rittelmeyer in Vienna, Carl was accepted into the founding circle of priests of the Christian Community, and was able to take part in their meetings in Breitbrunn, Germany. There he was asked to give a talk and chose to speak with great enthusiasm and engagment about the significance of the will forces slumbering in the workers. Carl Stegmann took on the religious work in the city of Hamburg with such energy, committment, and determination that Rudolf Steiner sent these words to him through a friend: "Tell him: such a fiery spirit we can really use in our movement."

The seeds planted in Carl Stegmann in Vienna came to fruition in 1927 when he took on the work in the city of Essen which is part of the Ruhr district, well known for its coal and steel output. There Carl could transform his strong social impulses and his deep interest in the working people into reality. He opened a "Workers' School" where he gathered unemployed workers who were seeking for answers. The Threefold Social Order in the widest sense was the starting point for all activities in this school. From there also the magazine *Decision* was published. Carl's purpose for both the school and the magazine was to guide the will forces of the young workers away from materialism, Darwinism, and Marxism to the idealism of Fichte, Goethe, Schelling, and Novalis so that through this they could find an openness to the spirit.

Carl found in the working class of that time vibrant energy, a youthful enthusiasm, a vitality, and the openness necessary to change and transform society. Carl had a unique way of combining practical work such as furniture manufacturing with continuing education, Anthroposophical studies and artistic endeavors. This flourishing school was closed by the Nazis in 1933. Carl had been under surveillance for some time and was finally arrested. He always recalled one of the Nazi officers saying, "We'll send you to a concentration camp so you will finally learn to work." Though he escaped that fate at that time, his further work was forbidden.

Though Carl and Christine Stegmann moved to Mannheim, the harassment of the family by the Nazis continued until 1941, when the Christian Community was officially forbidden and Carl was again arrested and imprisoned for his "subversive activities" which anything having to do with Anthroposophy and the Christian Community was considered to be.

After the war he put his total energy and efforts into rebuilding the Anthroposophical Society and the Christian Community in Mannheim. At that time also, he often spoke to us children about his wish to go to America. This wish became stronger and stronger, until in 1967 at the age of 70 it was possible for him to visit me, his youngest daughter then living in Oakland, California. He recalled this first visit to America later on in a letter:

> When I was here in America for the first time . . . I had the distinct feeling of a world that had much more behind it than the outer picture revealed. Looking back, I would characterize it in this way . . . I felt as if surrounded by youthful, socially open soul forces, by germinating activity forces that found their strongest expression in the economic life. These feelings accompanied all my impressions like a hidden music, at times softly, at times more distinctly, telling of the future possibilities of this continent.

In 1970 Carl Stegmann moved permanently to this country to begin his work here in California. He brought with him the rich experience of his long quest which was to deepen his understanding of the spiritual task of America in the threefold world. His intensive studies of American literature, philosophy, psychology, and political evolution which he had already begun long before in Germany were now continued with tremendous vigor and dedication. To awaken an understanding for the "inner, hidden potential of America" not only in the United States but also in Europe was his greatest wish. As he said in his "Essay on America" (1967):

If more and more people would recognize that there exists an 'inner America' and what this consists of—as seen through Anthroposophy—then this would already be working against the spiritual counter forces which can only flourish in an outer materialistic America.

When he, together with others, founded the Center for Anthroposophical Studies in 1976 (later named Rudolf Steiner College), he had already given many courses, lectured extensively and written several books to uncover the "inner spiritual America." In this book, *The Other America,* Carl Stegmann brought together his insights gained out of his lifelong quest.

Carl Stegmann crossed the threshold of death on February 16, 1996. We hope he will be pleased that his work is now coming home to America.

We are grateful to Thomas Stöckli for his editing of earlier text to form the unified version which was published in German in 1991, and to Maria St.Goar for her thoughtful translation of that text into English.

Astrid Schmitt-Stegmann
Fair Oaks, California 1997

PREFACE TO THE GERMAN EDITION

This study was originally brought out by the author in manuscript form in 1975/76. It is now published again in a new version that was edited by the author himself and Thomas Stöckli. Warm thanks go to Elisabeth Bessau for her valuable help in proofreading. We would also like to thank Harald Kiczka for assisting with the appendix about R. W. Emerson.

As Carl Stegmann states in the preface, his texts require a working knowledge of anthroposophical spiritual science. His resolute recounting of remarks by Rudolf Steiner on the subject of the West and America—which to him is synonymous with the United States of America—challenges readers to test and judge for themselves the veracity of these comments. In order to emphasize this attitude, one that in itself is always presupposed in Anthroposophy, this new edition is published as "study material." We hope that, in view of the challenges of the present and near future, the questions raised in this book will stimulate and encourage renewed work on finding answers.

Thomas Stöckli

PREFACE (1991)

The first publication of this study in 1975/76 happened to coincide with the bicentennial celebration of America's declaration of independence. The first century of American history may be viewed as establishing its physical constitution, as developing its "body." The second century can be seen to represent the cultural development or formation of a "soul." Finally, in the third century, the threshold to the "spirit" must be crossed. This is a critical phase of development. My aim at that time was to contribute to the advancement of spirituality. Some friends and I wished to help plant a seed that can bear fruit in the third century of United States history. This was the context in which I then placed this publication.

Now, my book, *The Other America*, appears in a new form. I was able to discuss this new version thorourghly with the editor, Thomas Stöckli, and would like to thank him as well as Elisabeth Bessau and Harald Kiczka for their contributions.

What global events surround this republication? The beginning of this year saw a formidable war between the USA (and their "allies") and Iraq. This conflict caused profound changes, especially when we are conscious of the spiritual dimension of events. Much is presently coming to the surface that was only barely discernable fifteen years ago. Rudolf Steiner's indications concerning the end of the century, a time we currently face, gain pressing actuality. May the following reflections aid orientation and compel motivation to strengthen the "spiritual America" by means of Rudolf Steiner's spiritual science, at a time when the terrifying, distorted image of America likewise tries to push to the surface.

Carl Stegmann
Mannheim, February 1991

PART I

INTRODUCTION

These reflections on the "inner appearance" and spiritual mission of America within the whole of humanity were addressed to persons familiar with Anthroposophy. Only those who have studied Anthroposophy for some time will be able to understand this text.

On different occasions, Rudolf Steiner spoke of pitfalls, talents, and tasks of the West. I have tried to form a clear picture of these. However, my interest in this subject did not date from the time I began to live in America. It started when I first became acquainted with the idea of the threefold social order[1] and was further deepened through my participation in the West-East Congress of 1922 in Vienna.[2] The concept of the threefold social order increases our comprehension of events that affect humanity in the East, in Central Europe, and in the West. Moreover, it facilitates an awareness of the various strengths and tasks of these regions.

These ideas motivated me to found a school for workers in the Ruhr Valley, in Germany. The school existed from 1928 until 1933 when it was forbidden by the Nazis. Several hundred young workmen attended and graduated from the full-time courses during those years. Among those who spoke there, were men like Roman Boos, Friedrich Rittelmeyer, Emil Bock, Gottfried Husemann, Zeylmans van Emmichoven, and Jürgen von Grone. Many of Rudolf Steiner's lectures were studied in detail in those days.

The many years of preoccupation with these matters eventually led to the expositions that follow in this book. Christine

1

Stegmann, with her broad knowledge of Anthroposophy and experience with young Americans in her Eurythmy courses, helped me greatly in this endeavor.

Carl Stegmann, 1975

THE AMERICAN DREAM

What comes to expression when people speak of the "American way of life?" They refer to something special, even if each person gives it a different interpretation. Or what is meant if, as is frequently done, one speaks of the "American dream?" It is the feeling that something was at work at the founding of America that was "not of this world," something that arose out of the primal creative dreams of the world, out of forces working unbeknown to human beings. A creative dream can rise up at any time in suitable individuals, and has indeed emerged in them. These individuals spoke about it, sometimes indistinctly or just fragmentally, without fully knowing of what they spoke; others—writers, poets, philosophers, religious leaders, business people, and politicians— were quite deliberate and clear about it.

Here are a few examples.[3] Charles Reich stated in *The Greening of America*: "The American dream was not, least of all in the beginning, a form of narrow materialism."

In a sermon, published in *The American Dream*, Peter Marshall said:

> What has America to give the rest of the world? If only grain, money, clothing or armaments, then we have already lost the war and the peace. . . . We have to give more, and I do not mean more dollars. I do not mean more tractors, I do not mean more guns! We have to give more, . . . namely our ideals, our faith, our philosophy of life, our concept of human dignity, our Bill of Rights, our American dream.

3

Thomas Wolfe wrote in *You Can't Go Home Again*:

> I believe that we here in America are lost, but I
> also believe that we shall be found again. . . . I think
> the true discovery still lies ahead of us. I think the
> true fulfillment of our spirit . . . is yet to come.

It is significant to note what a former Commissioner for
Indian Affairs, John Collier, writes in his book about Native
Americans and their spiritual beliefs:

> The real reason for the desperate condition of our
> world is that we have lost our passion and awe for the
> human personality and for the eternal living inter-
> change between life and the earth. This was some-
> thing the Indians of America guarded as the central,
> holy fire ever since the Stone Age. Our distant hope
> must therefore be to rekindle this holy fire in all of us.
> This is our only lasting hope.

Russell W. Davenport, who encountered Anthroposophy
during World War II, had two main goals in life, namely, to
work ceaselessly for the freedom of the human personality
and, secondly, to search out ever more deeply the actual mission of America. He was convinced that more is implied with
the phrase, "The American Dream," than people generally
think. One ought to look not only at what people say about it,
but also at what may have been spiritually active at the founding of a new nation in which representatives of all countries
came together. Davenport wrote in *The Dignity of Man*:

> A task lies ahead of America of truly overwhelm-
> ing proportions: the task of learning to inquire into the
> nature and destiny of man in a new way, of which our
> current spirit of inquiry has not yet dreamed. It sug-

gests the possibility of knowledge that we do not yet have, of vistas we have not yet opened up. And it intimates, finally, vistas we might find, not merely the solution to the American dilemma, but the foundations for an Idea of a Free Man.

It is essential that there are people who are able to recognize the true, effective forces active in and behind the West. It was absolutely clear to Davenport that this is possible only through Anthroposophy. Rudolf Steiner pointed out that Westerners, particularly Americans, live in the will, even when they think and investigate. He stated: "Above all in American literature, we regularly find that human will is referred to as the underlying motivating force."

The entire future of humankind lies hidden in the will. Rudolf Steiner says of America that a relatively simplistic view of the world exists there, but that this view "contains uncommon seeds for the future."[4] He makes it clear that an understanding must come about between the new European spirituality on the one hand and America on the other, so that America can find her own unique path. This path is still hidden today. If the forces active in America were to remain on the unconscious level, only harm could result from them. What is not grasped consciously falls prey to the opposing powers.

But we can struggle to become aware of the inner spiritual powers that manifest here in outer events. We can become aware of Western humanity's will-capabilities and their inherent potential. We can become conscious of the task of the West and what opposes it. Then, not only a new world would be revealed, that would otherwise remain hidden, but it will begin to become a reality.

ESSENTIAL QUESTIONS
REGARDING THE WESTERN WORLD

One of Rudolf Steiner's thoughts that can accompany us throughout these deliberations like an underlying theme is the following:

> An ever greater contrast will appear in the Anglo-American culture between men and women. Anglo-American spiritual life will . . . be passed on to future generations through womanhood. Those who live in male bodies, on the other hand, will strive for the ideas such as I have described.

Rudolf Steiner had explained that, due to their one-sided disposition of will, American manhood would produce a purely materialistic, increasingly mechanistic civilization. The life of feelings and the spirit would slowly be repressed. Women, on the other hand, who play an important role in America, will develop a faculty that will enable them to open themselves to a life of spirit and culture due to their disposition centered in the rhythmic human nature, in the heart. This will help them to attain the possibility of influencing American civilization in a spiritual way, thus adding a spiritual viewpoint to the materialistic, earthly-mechanistic one.

Two possible developments are indicated here. The first grows out of manhood, out of the intellect and will. The second can arise out of womanhood when the heart is spiritualized and is able to generate healing forces. The male population can become too closely identified with the earth and experience the body as totally connected to it, instinctively feeling:

"I am the gravity that passes through my legs; I am the weight that weighs down my hands and arms."[5]

Through manhood and womanhood, we are able to observe two life-streams that can turn into a picture which becomes more meaningful the longer we look at it. Lightning-like, this picture can illuminate the inner condition of this continent. We take note of the tragic inner struggle that rages unconsciously in the depths of American souls between earth's fetters and spirit longing. This is basically a battle that is being waged everywhere on earth since the end of the 19th century. It is the battle between the forces of Michael, who wishes to bring about the breakthrough of the heart's spiritualized thinking, and the Ahrimanic opposing forces, who, since that time, try one-sidedly to strengthen the head's intellectual thinking and the will's instinctive urges on earth.

In his lectures of 1922 in Vienna, Rudolf Steiner spoke of the different qualities of soul in the East, Central Europe and the West. In the East, the spirit is the determinant factor, in the Center, the soul, in the West, the body. While the East considers the spirit to be true reality and the sense world as Maya, the West today views the physical world as real and the spirit as ideology; Central Europe stands between these two.

In the same lectures, Rudolf Steiner also spoke of the interest of Americans in the labor movements. In the early days of the movement for the threefold social order immediately following World War I, Rudolf Steiner explained how the middle class (the bourgeoisie) is connected to the nerve-and-senses system, hence to thinking; how the aristocracy was predisposed to the rhythmic system, hence more to feeling; and how the working class with its qualities of the will is rooted in the metabolic-limb system. And Western humanity likewise has this disposition, living as it does in the metabolic-limb system. Rudolf Steiner felt that a proper understanding of the working class was most important. For he saw workers as representatives of future humanity in whom the will would be dominant. In those days he often said that people should not think *about* the working class but rather *with* them. What does it mean to think *with* them? We should not face workers as spectators; we should think with them from inside them. I believe this quote is likewise applicable to Western humanity. We should not think *about* America, but in accordance with her inner being. This is quite a different way of gaining insight; this insight penetrates into the depths.

In turn, this leads to an important question: How do persons, in whom metabolism and will predominate, find their way to the spiritual world? This is not a hypothetical question, not only a matter of knowledge, but an essential question. I would like to clarify this by a verse from the Mystery Plays. In *The Soul's Awakening*, Benedictus, Maria, and Ahriman are gathered around Strader. As we know, Strader for the most part pursues a Western path. He has had to listen to bitter truths, but then Maria says to him:

> While Felix tempers for himself the weapons
> Which shield him against danger, —one who walks
> Your paths of soul must use another kind.
> The sword Capesius forges for himself
> And bravely wields in battle with his foes
> Must change for Strader to a shadow-sword[6] ···

Strader has to follow his own direction, not the path of Felix Balde or Capesius. This is what it is basically all about, namely, that we do not hold a mere shadow-sword in our hands when the decisive events begin at the turn of the century. Western humanity has to forge its own sword out of its own inner impulse and out of what spiritual science has to offer.

The Way to the West

When a European comes to America for the first time, it is a surprising fact to realize from one's own experience that people of all nations have come together here. Although I had obviously known this, it was quite amazing to see representatives from lands the world over gathered together with all their differences. No other country on earth represents the whole of humanity the way North America does. If you are the least bit receptive to the workings of higher powers of destiny, this becomes a serious question: Why does all of humanity flock together in America? Certainly, any number of reasons can be given for this. Yet, viewed from an inner level, one confronts a profound riddle. Some have had a feeling for this.

The urge to move to the Western hemisphere from all over the world did not originate in the head but in the unconscious human will, in the sphere where the will, as if asleep, is still connected with the spirit of the cosmos. The Californian, John Steinbeck, pointed to this connection. He was particularly sympathetic to those who labor with their hands, and clearly noticed the antisocial conditions in America. In him, this combined with a subtle feeling for the workings of supersensible forces. In his book, *The Red Pony*, he has an old Westerner speak about the first settlers who came to America:

> There were bunches of people who were grown together into one great big creeping beast. . . . It was the migration to the West. Everybody wanted something for himself, but the big beast made up of us all just wanted to go West. I was a guide, but if I hadn't

been, then somebody else would have been the head man. The beast had to have a head.[7]

One realizes that he did not consider individual personal desires of people to be the essential thing. It was something that was not visible to external eyes, an invisible creature, a supersensible group-being in need of a "head" on earth. This spirit that pressed toward the West sought to create a body for itself in America.

F. W. Zeylmans van Emmichoven likewise draws attention to this spirit of the West.

> Those who first emigrated to the United States, the British, French, Spaniards, and Dutchmen, belonged to old, already then distinctive folk groups. If they encountered forces here that influenced even them, members of older nations, forces that could form a new, young people out of them, then these forces must have a profound effect and be of a quite different kind than the forces of old nations. For sure, the above-mentioned powers above and below earth's surface supply part of the explanation, but there is more to it than just this.[8]

Compared to the older nations, America is still a young country. It was discovered, or rediscovered, in the 15th century, when the development of the consciousness soul began. England assumed the leading role in this evolution of the consciousness soul, while America was as yet coming into being. The current threefold order of East, West, and Center arose out of the migration to America. North America became the actual representative of the West. England is an important Western country, but her people, being a European nation, are linked to the spirit of the Center. Important anthroposophical topics were proclaimed by Rudolf Steiner in England as well. In Vienna, he spoke in 1922 about the East, about Europe as the Middle, and America as the West.

Through the workings of destiny, human beings with a marked potential of will were drawn together in America. They were persons whose metabolic-limb system was strong. On the one hand, the people of the United States are a people like any other; on the other, they are something quite different. The population is not united by common blood. Through it flows the blood of many nations and races. Here, humanity is gathered together. We can decipher the mission of this population from this fact. It must come to know itself and its unique characteristics. It must recognize its talents, possibilities, and its mission within the whole of humanity.

MYSTERIES OF THE WILL

The preponderance of will in the American people is noticeable without any dificulties. Zeylmans van Emmichoven writes:

> It was the youngest and yet most powerful force of the human soul, namely the will, that drove people, irrespective of their country of origin, to America. Whether it was the will to turn religious ideals in freedom into reality, the will to escape tyranny, the will to create a more favorable economic existence or the will to confront the great unknown: It was always the will, meaning, the most unconscious, least formed, and yet strongest soul force.[9]

We are indeed least conscious of the will. I can entertain the thought that I wish to open the window. In order actually to do this, my will must set my limbs in motion. What happens inside me when the will moves my limbs remains hidden from me. Yet it is one of the great tasks in the West to recognize the true nature of the will.

Walter Bühler offers an example of how the will can be traced back from consciousness to the unconscious.[10] He outlines how the will that moves our limbs also works in our digestion. When we eat food, we begin by chewing and salivating; we move the food back and forth with our tongue and then swallow it. We can follow this process consciously up to the point where the chewed food glides down the esophagus, but no further, even though the dissolution of the food continues in the stomach, intestines, and blood. We realize how the process that is initiated by consciousness is continued by the will, which remains unconscious. This unconscious will, which is active in all the mysterious digestive processes of transformation, is likewise the force behind motion in human limbs. The spiritual world's purity, its selfless power of giving live in this will, which remains unconscious to us. During the night, human beings through their will are one with the cosmic world-will and experience the former's moral-spiritual force.

One of the greatest mysteries of world evolution is that the highest spirit and soul forces, if cut off from their cosmic origin, turn into their opposite in earthly human beings. This is the mystery of Cain. The moral power of giving is then changed into ruthless self-assertion; the spiritual will to become one with the world and its creatures turns into anti-social, divisive will that splits up a community. The will of self-sacrifice is transformed into the will to sacrifice and destroy one's fellow human beings. Yet, such insight is not merely depressing. It is comforting as well, for what came out of the spirit, even if it was darkened, can be transformed once again into spirit. In all that is negative, seeds for the future are contained. We could not work on earth without the certainty that the world's evil can be transformed into good through insight and love.

Rudolf Steiner draws our attention to yet another significant aspect. When the human soul ascends after death into higher spheres of existence, then, first and foremost, human consciousness changes. We then attain to an ever brighter, more comprehensive, will-imbued, cosmic consciousness. We gradually become one with the cosmos and our own spirit-being. Eventually, there comes the descent into a new earthly life. A reverse process then takes place. When we descend to a new incarnation on earth, we lose the brightness and breadth of our cosmic consciousness in stages. Shortly before we unite with the germ of an embryo, our consciousness is totally dimmed. Thus released, the spiritual energies of consciousness are transformed into growth forces of the developing human being:

> There, where we received a first enlightenment for the supersensible world in a more alert consciousness than we are able to possess on earth, there, on our return to earth, consciousness is dimmed until it is diminished so far that it can become only a force of growth. . . .[11]

The inner relationship between life and consciousness is thus uncovered. It is of particular importance that life and growth processes are related to will forces:

> All growth that proliferates in us is at the same time related to will. Seen externally in the body, it is a growth process. Observed in the inner soul life, it is will. This brings us to the conclusion that the proliferation of growth, everything that in any way is inherent within these forces that come to expression in growth, digestion, in life generally, is will-related. When we observe this from the point of view of the soul, we must say that it is connected to the will.[12]

Here we come close to the mystery of the will. Will is life and life is metamorphosed higher consciousness. If one bears this in mind, then, here in America, one thinks immediately of the land as such with its rich primordial growth forces. Everyone knows that giant trees exist here that were growing even at the time of Christ. You can carve a tunnel into them large enough for cars to drive through. Where powerful growth forces are at work in the human being, such as in the small child, there is little consciousness. Initially, a child lives totally in the will-imbued powers that build up the body. He, she, only gradually awakens to consciousness, to the degree that the growth forces withdraw from the body. This confirms in a wonderful way that growth forces are transformed into forces of consciousness.

When we realize how our will extends–for our perception unconsciously–into the creative, spiritual will forces, we can arrive at the invigorating certainty in waking day-consciousness that, in all its growth processes, in all the mysterious ways of its digestion, in all movements of its limbs, our physical body is permeated by the highest spiritual powers. Added to this is the equally significant knowledge, namely, that every night we ascend to spiritual spheres in order to be immersed in an exalted spiritual-moral world, a world where will, love, and consciousness are one. Here we experience our cosmic human state, our higher, spiritual "I". We can cause our earthly human nature to unite gradually with our cosmic "I" by illuminating the depths of our will with thoughts of the spirit. Without the light of cognition, the noblest social forces remain nothing but blind instincts; they slip away from us and are then seized by opposing Ahrimanic forces. If the will is recognized, it will be retained for the West and saved for humanity.

Thinking and its Antisocial Effect

Rudolf Steiner pointed out that American culture is essentially formed out of intellect and will, not out of the forces of the human middle. It is impossible to understand the outer events of our time without seeing the power that gives them their characteristic feature, namely thinking. Thinking turned increasingly to an exploration of the earth, developed present-day science with its great discoveries and technology, and resulted in modern industry. Thinking changed the face of the earth. Yet, because of the evolving intellect, it cut human beings off from their spiritual origin. Humanity is unable to recognize the spiritual in the world. This is the negative side of today's abstract thinking. This thinking has the power to lead each human being to his/her personality by unfolding a new self-awareness, but it individualizes so strongly that it has an antisocial effect, dissolving communities and separating people from each other. Take a remark by Rudolf Steiner from 1919:

> If you allow the present form of teaching to continue at our universities for three more decades and permit the present mode of thinking about social questions to go on for thirty more years, you will have a devastated Europe thirty years hence.[13]

The astounding thing about this remark is that Rudolf Steiner directly connects our way of thinking with social events; that he dares make a prediction based on it, and that the prediction is accurate. Thirty years later, in 1949, humanity had just gone through the Second World War. The war had turned Europe into a pile of rubble and became the cause for all the events that we today experience at a growing rate as acts of violence and terrorism.

We accomplish little in the social realm when we know theoretically that the changing consciousness is the cause of all transformations in the outer world. It was just this modern manner of thinking referred to by Rudolf Steiner that was adopted in a particular way by Marxism and applied to economic and social conditions, which had come to the fore in recent times. By so doing, Marxism arrived at a view opposite that of Rudolf Steiner, namely, that no world-transforming reality is inherent in thinking consciousness; that it has only an ideological character. The determining factors of social life were seen by Marxism to be contained in economic conditions of property and holdings. Yet, although we live today in an age where we have to deal with deadened thoughts, we can still endow them with effective power. Marxism itself even proves this. First, it was a theory, a structure of thoughts created by Marx and Engels. Then, many thousands of workers became familiar with these thoughts, thoughts that are not easily grasped. But the workers thought them through again and again and thereby strengthened them. These thoughts spread out, turned into a force that cried out for realization, and became reality in Russia in 1917. We see that Marxism first existed as thought and only after that became historical fact. Even Marxism, contrary to its own view, proves that all historical developments have their beginning in thinking. If we make this clear to ourselves, we can be absolutely certain that all events, even social and economic ones, proceed from thinking, that is, from the human spirit.

Shortly before Karl Marx, the philosopher and sociologist Auguste Comte lived in France. Out of an inner affinity for the spirit, he asserted the opposite of Karl Marx's idea. He stated that it is man's spirit that shapes life on earth, not withstanding that spirit for him meant positivistic thinking. He spoke of three states of development. First, there was the stage of pure theological thinking. Then followed the stage of metaphysical thinking, and finally that of positivistic thinking. He sought for the law that causes new thinking in each case to prevail against all odds until events of the time become a manifestation of said thinking. All outer events, be it in science, art, religion, education, economics, or social life, are then an accurate revelation and symptom of that one mode of thinking that underlies them all.

Even though Comte clearly recognized the history-producing power of human consciousness, he succumbed to an illusion. He was convinced that, if positivistic thinking were to gain acceptance and fully imbue humanity, such a thinking would produce an impact that could reconcile people and link soul with soul. He felt that such a thinking could give rise to a sort of universal human religion.

Today, we realize that this thinking cannot produce a harmonizing moral force that socially unites people. On the contrary, it is a force that individualizes and isolates us. It encapsulates us in ourselves and separates us from others. We have lost the ability of uniting with other souls to the point where we can understand them from within; otherwise there would not be so many arguments, fights, and indeed wars between people and nations. This thinking atomizes humanity, splits it into ethnic groups concerned only about their own needs, and into countless egocentrically thinking and acting individuals.

The antisocial power of today's thinking and its propensity to arouse argument and confrontation was recognized later on by another Frenchman, Gabriel Marcel.[14] He identified the effect inherent in the abstract nature of today's thinking, a thinking through which we are never led to an actual individual person and to what goes on in his or her mind, but invariably to an abstract image of man. We speak of the Englishman, the Russian, the German, the American. But *the* Englishman, *the* Russian, *the* Norwegian does not exist anywhere, only individual human beings with their own unique characteristics and talents. No one has ever encountered "the" Englishman or "the" American. They are abstractions. We are surrounded by abstractions. We speak of the Christian, the Muslim, the Communist, the Catholic, the Protestant. These abstractions separate us from reality. Marcel states that this abstract thinking is the cause of our mutual estrangement, our anti-religious life, but most of all the reason for antisocial behavior, for argument and conflicts between nations and people.

Rudolf Steiner said concerning human beings:

> Above all, we humans are not simple beings, even in regard to social relationships. Especially in the social regard, we are beings we would rather *not* be at all; we would infinitely prefer to be different than we are. One can say that basically we love ouselves very much. . . And it is because of this self-love that we turn self-knowledge into a source of illusion. We do not wish to admit that only half of our being is social and that in our other half we are quite antisocial.

One of the basic criteria for human interaction is, therefore, for every single person to recognize that he or she harbors antisocial inclinations. And this is connected with our thinking. Rudolf Steiner continues:

In regard to perceptions and thinking, we must above all clearly understand that these perceptions and thinking contain a tremendously significant source of human antisocial behavior. Inasmuch as we are thinking human beings, we are antisocial beings.[15]

With this in mind, we ought to observe ourselves. Then we will become quite convinced of the truth of this statement. With a certain horror, we will discover the activity of an antisocial power in ourselves, which, to begin with, far outweighs all social inclination.

Current antisocial thinking individualizes human beings. And thus begins the development of becoming an independent person, of acquiring consciousness of self, something that must develop in everyone today. It is part of the tragedy of humanity's evolution that we have to pay for the attainment of our independence, our individual personality, by developing a consciousness that releases antisocial forces. We can clearly see how one person's thinking leads to criticism of another, who in turn feels rebuffed. This thinking arouses antipathy in feeling which then hurts the other person. It generates hatred in the will that can lead to murder, as with Cain.

In contrast to this, love rises out of the will's depths, if will is not corrupted. This love is transformed to sympathy in feeling, the middle or central aspect of the human being. In the head organization, it changes into positive acknowledgment of the other individual. Will is initially social in us. In the sleeping depths of our will we are always connected with the universal spirit and united with all beings, even if we are not conscious of this by day. The social efforts of the human soul arise out of the will.

One who is sensitive to this would have been able to experience it clearly in Central European laborers when they were amongst themselves. One can moreover experience it today in America in the often amazing, natural human fellowship. One can sense the presence of a primeval, seed-like social force that, as yet, has not matured to full reality, because it is not yet being illuminated by the light of consciousness. A truly genuine social force existed in the beginning among the working-classes. But the more this force passed over into thinking through Marxism, the more other forces gained the upper hand.

Strong religious movements exist in America. If one looks at what they try to accomplish, it is often astonishing how clearly the will can reveal its social quality in the religious field. Religious people want to put love into practice; they try to meet others with warm sympathy. They do not seek the splinter in the others' eye nor speak disparagingly of them. They do not choose to live alone and isolated only for themselves but in communities. They want to *live* religion, study the Bible. But they do have an aversion to becoming too involved in thinking, as though they had an instinctive fear that recognition would change all-too-easily into negative criticism, sympathy into antipathy, love into love of self and hatred of other people. Some religious people are afraid of consciousness!

The antisocial element of thinking becomes even clearer when one reads what Rudolf Steiner had to say about it. In human interaction, one tries to lull the other to sleep, as it were, not in the domains of feeling and will but in that of thinking:

> ... It is a peculiar fact that, inasmuch as you confront another person as an imagining, thinking being,

the desire is present in your subconsciousness to be lulled to sleep by the other, simply through the mutual relationship that forms between one person and another. You are lulled to sleep, as it were, by the other in your subconsciousness. This is the normal relationship between two people. When we come together, one is always trying to lull the subconsciousness of the other to sleep—of course, it works both ways. And what do you therefore have to do as a thinking being? Of course, everything I am telling you takes place in the subconsciousness. . . . You must inwardly defend yourself against this, if you wish to remain a thinking person. You have to activate your thinking. You have to defend yourself against going to sleep.[16]

Why do I try to lull the other person to sleep? Because his or her thinking opposes me, because thinking is antisocial, critical, filled with antipathy and aggression. I try to eliminate *this* being, so that the social being, the social will in him or her can come to life and agree with me and do what *I* want. This does occur unconsciously, but when we become alert to it, we can observe it wherever people come together, as friends, as married couples, coworkers, as participants in a discussion. Everywhere, originating from thinking, an unconscious battle ensues. It can be observed in the larger social contexts, very clearly of course in dictatorships. With speeches that have a suggestive effect, with blatant propaganda that is ruthlessly repeated constantly, the population's consciousness is meant to be reduced to sleep. It is astounding that most people have a tendency to let themselves be lulled to sleep. For then they do not have to be against anything, they do not have to stand up for their own opinion; they can sleep in peace. Naturally, it goes without saying that many others oppose any attempt at being lulled to sleep.

25

If we picture this covert struggle between people, we clearly see that a socially connecting bond between individuals cannot grow out of today's thinking. Just the opposite will result: a community-destroying element, brought about by steadily worsening, eroding criticism, and by hostility provoking antipathies and hatred. These urge one on to acts of violence in the battle for self-assertion between individuals, groups, peoples, and nations. This is a picture of our time.

Now we can fully understand Rudolf Steiner's passage that was quoted earlier:

> If you allow the present form of teaching to continue at our universities for three more decades and permit the present mode of thinking about social questions to go on for thirty more years, you will have a devastated Europe thirty years hence.

Presently, this devastation affects the whole world. Rudolf Steiner continues:

> You can propose as many ideals as you like in this or that field. You can talk about various questions raised by this or that group of people until you are blue in the face. You can speak in the belief that something can be done for humanity's future by voicing urgent demands. All will be in vain if the transformation does not come about out of the very foundations of the human soul; out of thinking about the connection of this world to the spiritual world. Humanity must develop a new thinking . . . for the evils of our time issue from our perverted spiritual life.[17]

If we can say this with an inner conviction acquired by our own efforts, the following perception arises in the soul: Now I stand on firm ground; from here I can try to understand the social problems of our age. I know with certainty that no good can come to humanity, if the lever is not applied in the area where the source of today's disintegration lies, i.e. in our present-day thinking. To be sure, we have to remember that this thinking brought us our freedom. We may no longer be controlled by powers working from outside, as was the case in ancient times. We even have to credit the antisocial forces separating us from others for our development into individual beings. We isolate ourselves from others, close ourselves off in ourselves. We become individualized. We have to assert ourselves against others who criticize us and even develop hostility and hate against us. Achieving our own free and strong personality is often an arduous undertaking. The antisocial forces in the world are as necessary for humanity's proper evolution as are the social ones. If, in the age of the consciousness soul, we wanted only to activate our social forces here on earth, we would fall asleep. A balance has to be established between the social and antisocial forces.

At this point, I would like to take a look at the revolutionary segment of American youth in order to illustrate what I have just said by means of a concrete, well-known example. Strong social impulses exist in today's young people, especially among college students, impulses that unconsciously rise up from the depths of their spirit-related will. On the other side, a thinking imbues them that is acquired at the universities. And so they live in the conflict between social and antisocial forces. Especially the students who are social revolutionaries—and they need not always be Marxists—quite strongly experience the unsocial, inhuman aspects of contemporary civilization. Their social sensibility encounters a world that is a manifestation of antisocial thinking in all its institutions and events. As meaningful as this thinking is on the one hand, it cannot but have antisocial effects.

Although the following episode occurred some time back, I would nonetheless like to mention it because it is symptomatic for much that goes on under the surface in American social life. It is the true story of Patty Hearst, the daughter of a newspaper publisher in San Francisco. The Hearst family is one of the best-known, richest families in America. Patty Hearst attended the University of California at Berkeley and lived there in a small house. One day she was kidnapped by a social-revolutionary group. This group admittedly had shot and killed a prominent school-superintendent in Oakland for political reasons. Patty Hearst's kidnapping disturbed all of America. Everyone thought the group would demand a high ransom to further their own revolutionary aims. As was later discovered, the group consisted mainly of non-Marxist, but revolutionary, students from good families. They demanded an enormous sum, in order to supply the indigent population of California with groceries. If the Hearst family would not comply, their daughter would be killed. By means of a recording forwarded to them that was moreover broadcast on TV, she herself implored her parents to fulfill the demand and save her life. An agreement of several million dollars was reached. Food distribution took place in several locations across California and thousands flocked there to receive supplies. Subsequently, Patty Hearst was supposed to be released. Then came the totally unexpected news that shocked so many: Patty Hearst did not wish to be released. Instead, she hoped to become a member of this revolutionary group. On a new recording, that was likewise broadcast, she explained her reasons. Henceforth, she intended to oppose the present American establishment, defend the victims of this society, and stand up for those who could not help themselves. She disavowed her own parents and wanted nothing more to do with their wealth. She assumed a new name and turned into an active member of this group. She was not present when, a few weeks later, the six most important leaders of the group were trapped in a house in Los Angeles in a confrontation with the police and were either shot or burned to death in the building that had caught on fire. Patty Hearst herself remained in hiding.

Such a tragic case affords quite an insight into the events of our time and youth's state of mind. Powerful social impulses are rising from the depth of will; they are repressed, obscured, or perverted by the thinking learned today. Based on genuine social impulses, young people feel called upon to help, yet see no other way than that of using force, terror, and murder. They are unable to perceive the true causes of present-day social ills. They do not recognize what is at work in the depths of their will, nor are they aware that contemporary thinking must be transformed and that their life of heart and feeling is more or less being crushed by this culture.

What happens when unchanged thinking and will clash with each other without the harmonizing power of the heart? America itself offers a clear answer to this. The mountain ranges in America all run from north to south. The cold Arctic winds stream down unhindered into the warm South. In the Gulf of Mexico, they meet the hot air that streams northward. Where they clash together, terrible whirlwinds ensue, hurricanes and tornadoes with their ravaging, all-destructive power. Similarly, the cold extreme of intellectual thinking must not strike unhindered upon the fire of the will, or else social whirlwinds of devastating power will result.

Rudolf Steiner saw this coming. He said something amazing about the end of the century:

> If things are allowed to continue on the course that I have described, a course that understandably

arose for the 20th century under the influence of the world view of the 19th century, then, at the end of the 20th century, we will face the war of all against all. All the splendid talks people may give and all scientific progress notwithstanding, we would still face this war of all against all.[18]

For the middle, or rhythmic, part of the human being is missing. Even as the rhythm of winter and summer, of death and life in the course of the year fit together to produce fruitful growth, so too it is the task of the center, the human rhythmic system, to bring the two extremes, death in thinking and life in the will, into beneficial, harmonious cooperation. But this does not happen by itself. For this, something must come to birth in the human being that is strong enough to generate balance, rhythm, and harmony. That is the higher ego in us.

THE STRUGGLE FOR
EGO-AWARENESS IN THE WEST

Rudolf Steiner depicted the archetype of the human ego or "I" in the statue of the Representative of Man, the one who can hold the balance between above and below, between thinking and willing, Lucifer and Ahriman, East and West. Unlike in a scale, balance is not brought about by shifting of weight but through a process of acquiring inner maturity, by actively transforming thinking, feeling, and willing, through the birth of the higher ego in the human being. This is comparable to the rising of a spiritual sun with its creative warmth and illuminating light. We aim for this in every meditation. In every meditation, we work on uniting the light of spiritual thoughts with the warming life-force of the will. Thought and will meet in the heart. The ego can then find its sphere of activity in an illuminated, enwarmed heart. The higher "I" is not merely the experience of a central point in the human being. It encompasses all of humanity, indeed, even the cosmic spirit. It has no self-interests, only concerns for humanity and the world.

Central Europe has a natural tendency to develop this ego. In the East, it exists more as spiritual, loving thinking; in Central Europe, the Middle, it emerges more from the enlightened feelings of the heart. It manifests as will-accentuated ego in the West. Ancient spirituality can be a hindrance for ego development in the East. What can freely unfold in the Middle must be won by effort in the West in the struggle with an all-too-powerful experience of earth and corporeality. In the East, the "I" has difficulty remaining awake in the powerful experience of sympathy and love. In the

Middle, it has to contend with sudden surges of sympathy and antipathy. The West has to develop the ego in the face of death's assaults. Rudolf Steiner once explained that the mysteries of birth and life are effective in the East. The mystery of life and death prevails in the Middle. The West has to figure out the mystery of death.[19] And in order to be able to recognize and master death, the secret of resurrection has to be uncovered.

In America, integration of all the representatives of humanity in one nation demands the search for the spirit of humanity which can unite them all. At the end of World War I, the old Austria-Hungary, an empire in which a number of different cultures had been united, broke apart. At that time, Rudolf Steiner said that Austria had had the mission of forming a union of diverse peoples, a union in which, without surrendering their particular cultural attributes, various nations could have lived together by virtue of a higher human element. Austria could not do it and thus disintegrated. There is no country on earth today where the necessity of attaining a common spirit transcending all narrow, nationalistic trends is as evident as in America. Here, common blood cannot be the unifying link. It matters not that we are English, Dutch, German, African, white, yellow, or red; what matters is that we are human beings.

We can only be human in our ego, in our higher "I" that envelops all humanity as well. Can traces of the higher ego be unearthed in this country that is so totally oriented toward technology and industry?

In his book, *Mr. Smith*, Louis Bromfield describes an encounter with this other ego.[20] He pictures the destiny of a man whose life all at once took a turn when he saw himself suddenly with new eyes one morning while shaving. Looking at himself in the mirror as if he were a stranger, he thought:

Is that you? Is that the person with whom you must live for the rest of your life? What are you? Are you decent and good or are you a monster? What do you want? Where do you want to go? . . . Where do you come from? . . . What are you here for? He remained standing for a long time, observing himself. Then something extraordinary happened. Everything in the room stayed as it had been before, and yet everything within him was totally different. He suddenly saw his life up to this point in another light. Its emptiness and senselessness became clear to him: "How should one describe it? Depression, monotony, futility, spiritual poverty?" He could not help but think of this again and again in the days that followed. He had to admit to himself: "It was not my ego, it was another ego that fascinated me and that I tried to figure out."

Bromfield calls Mr. Smith an average American. This experience of life's senselessness and emptiness is one that more and more Americans have, especially while they are young. Today, many of them experience the meaninglessness, spiritual poverty, and monotony of contemporary civilization with its ambitions for the high life and greater wealth. They sense that something is astir deep down in their souls, something completely different, that would like to break through. But they cannot grasp what it is. Today's education has given them no thoughts that could shed light on what is astir within them. It is the other ego, the ego that Mr. Smith has discovered in himself. Mr. Smith reflects often on what is going on within him: "I believe I can only describe it as an intense longing to explore what, in the final analysis, was I myself." Yet he cannot manage to find out about it. The thoughts are lacking that would enlighten him. What he then states concerning the futility of his search depicts the overwhelming tragedy of our age and characterizes its inner condition:

Well, so it went and I advise any and all never to start on such a course of inquiry, for it never stops as long as we live. It is even quite undeniable that, while the body dies and decomposes, we still have no assurance that the spirit, the ego, the soul, or whatever it is, dies with the body, or whether there is perhaps no end to this thing. Better to live like an animal, the way my sergeant does, whose only concerns are food, women, and enough money.

If we do not recognize what is stirring in the depths of our soul and tries to be born; if we do not know how it can be brought to birth—and this can be accomplished only based on spiritualized thoughts; the result will be a frightful devastation of soul, resignation, and despair. This ultimately leads to the craving for forms of sedatives. Materialism will proliferate. Instead of becoming imbued with the higher ego, human souls will increasingly bond with those earth-forces that drag them downward.

A book by Charles Reich affords profound insights into what goes on in the minds of young people in America. A professor at Yale University, he states in his introduction that he could not have written *The Greening of America* without the help of the hundreds of students with whom he had discussed these questions over and over again.[21] He is of the conviction that the state of human consciousness at any given time always determines the social, political, and cultural structure of an age: "From the start of this book, we have argued that consciousness plays the key role. . . ."

He tries to point out to the students that neither violent acts of terrorism nor revolutions will change anything in America, only the transformation and revolutionizing of consciousness. A new consciousness affects young people, one he somewhat abstractly calls Consciousness III. Initially, it lives in them as an unconscious, but powerful impulse of will. Members of the younger generation feel they confront a world that tries to rob them of their actual human state, tries to take from them their very ego. They have to defend themselves against this. Reich asks: What sort of life does a person lead today?

> It is like the life that was foreseen in *The Cabinet of Dr. Caligari, Metropolis,* and *M*, a robot life, in which man is deprived of his own being, and he becomes instead a mere role, occupation, or function. The self within him is killed. . . .

Reich carefully examines how America arrived at this situation and how young people rebelled against it. When the new consciousness, Consciousness III, awoke in the souls, it placed itself in opposition to the previous state of mind, Consciousness II.

> The foundation of Consciousness III is liberation. . . . The meaning of liberation is that the individual is free to build his own philosophy and values, his own life-style, and his own culture. . . . Consciousness III starts with self. In contrast to Consciousness II, which accepts society, the public interest and institutions as the primary reality, III declares that the individual self is the only true reality.

And Reich writes that this attitude is the fundamental impulse that lives in thousands of students and young people. He sees a danger for ego-evolution in the corporate state. He declares that we can no longer speak of capitalism, imperialism, or a power elite in America's economy today:

That, at least, would be a human shape. Of course a power elite does exist and is made rich by the system, but the elite are no longer in control, they are now merely taking advantage of forces that have a life of their own.

It is amazing that Reich can see this. Rudolf Steiner pointed out that, since the end of the 19th century, powers became active that develop a sort of life of their own so that people today no longer can exercise control of their own, over economic processes. A single personality cannot be effective anymore against the mechanism at work in economic operations. Charles Reich states that these arbitrary powers are effective everywhere in the world, but that in other nations more is at work than just this: "We have turned over everything, rendered ourselves powerless, and thus allowed mindless machinery to become our master."

If the ego that is struggling to come to light in human souls is not recognized for what it is, it disappears along with all the positive, good impulses at work in human beings today. Charles Reich realizes this in regard to young people. Deeply saddened, he observes the fact that many students lose their impulses and ideals as soon as they switch from the university to their professional life. His book makes it clear that a profound longing for taking hold of the ego imbues young people. Behind this impulse exists the "I" that arises out of the depths of soul.

Even in his age, Ralph Waldo Emerson could describe the ego, the "higher soul of man," in fitting words:

> It all goes to show that the soul of man is not an organ by itself, but enlivens and exercises all his organs. It is not a function as is the power of memory, the faculty for calculation and comparison. Rather, it

uses these as hands and feet. It is not a faculty but a source of light; it is not intellect or will but their master. It is the background of our existence in which all this is imbedded as in something immeasurable, unpossessed, and unpossessable. From within or from behind, a light shines through us.[22]

For Emerson, the earthly, visible human being "is merely the facade of a temple in which all wisdom and goodness dwell." The free and independent human ego, that works in the body and its organs, is moreover the master of our thinking and willing. It is the creative light that shines forth out of our spiritual foundation. With this, Emerson approaches the true, creative nature of the higher self. This higher ego furthermore encompasses the cosmos with its spiritual forces:

> The union of God and man in the soul's every action cannot be grasped in words. The simplest man who approaches God with an undivided heart becomes himself divine. Yet, the streaming in of this better and all-encompassing self is forever and eternally new and incomprehensible.

If human beings can thus rise above their ordinary self, a time of new ideas and new forces will surely come, says Emerson.

> More and more, the waves of eternal nature surge around me, and in all my relationships and actions I grow upwards into the all-human sphere. Thus I attain the level of living in ideas and working in energies that are immortal.

For Emerson, the "all-human" element was not just a word but reality. It is the soul of humanity that joins all single human beings into a unity.

Young people in America have a particularly strong leaning to Walt Whitman. Everyone is familiar with his great dramatic poem, *Song of Myself*. Why does youth incline so much to Whitman? Because he could say something about man's inner spiritual self, not with abstract thoughts but based on his own experience.

Song of Myself[23] does not immediately reveal its innermost substance. Yet it contains much which indicates that those are right who insist that this creation originated from personal spirit-vision. In the poem, he describes the awakening of the self in the human soul, its purification and enlightenment, its state of oneness with the divine in the world, and its reemergence from out of the spirit. Walt Whitman reveals something of the mystery of the will, which in its origin is "self" as well as "oneness" with all the world's beings:

> Swiftly arose and spread around me the peace and
> knowledge that pass all the argument of the earth,
> And I know that the hand of God is the promise of my
> own,
> And I know that the spirit of God is the brother of my
> own,
> And that all the men ever born are also my brothers,
> and the women my sisters and loving companions,
> And that a kelson of the creation is love.

It is important to realize that the great impulses—the struggle for the true self and the demand for spiritualization of will and thinking—arise out of the inner being of the West itself.

THE APOCALYPTIC SIGNIFICANCE
OF MICHAEL'S BATTLE

It is not possible to understand events on earth without looking into those occurrences that take place in the spiritual
world. What happens on earth between people and nations is
a result of spiritual happenings. And the impulses that arise
out of a person's depths of will point to impulses that come
from higher spiritual beings, regardless of whether they are in
the service of the good guiding powers or the world, or in the
service of powers that pursue other goals. In the present,
nothing can make this as clear as Michael's battle against the
opposing Ahrimanic powers. If this spirit-battle is used as a
key for understanding, our age and its events slowly become
transparent.

The year 1879 is the beginning of one of the most incisive
moments in humanity's evolution. At that time Michael, the
archangel of the Sun, who in pre-Christian times was in the
service of Yahweh, assumed rulership of the age. He had prepared for this task since the Mystery of Golgotha. Today, he
has placed himself completely in Christ's service. What he
proclaims to human beings is therefore at the same time a revelation of the goals of the Christ-being in our present time.
The mighty transition that hereby occurred lies in the fact
that the Moon-forces of Yahweh, that lingered on until the
middle of the 19th century, are being replaced at last by the
Sun-forces of the Christ. The forces manifesting in a folk,
those of blood and heredity through which Yahweh worked,
are replaced in the present by the Christ's spiritually and
etherically working lifeblood.[24] His etherized lifeblood works

effectivly in the creation of a new life of ideas, which is independent of all hereditary faculties.

In the service of the Christ, Michael has become the inspiring time-spirit for the three to four centuries following the year 1879. His activity already began in 1841 in the sphere of the spiritual world directly adjacent to the physical realm. Here, the opposing Ahrimanic powers gathered in order to prevent the beginning of this new, important phase of humanity's evolution, for they were pursuing their own goals. This led to a fierce battle in the supersensible world. It lasted for more than three decades, until Michael was able to cast these opponents of evolution down to earth, in order to free the supersensible sphere for the activity of the Christ reappearing etherically. With this began the most significant spirit-activity since the Mystery of Golgotha. It will lead humanity to entirely new possibilities in the course of its ongoing evolution.

Rudolf Steiner in this connection often referred to the 12th chapter of Revelations, where the battle of Michael with the dragon-forces is depicted. In the higher worlds, John beheld a majestic spirit-picture, a mighty imagination. In the sphere of the Sun, the figure of a woman took on form. She had placed the Moon with its forces under her feet. On her head, she bore a crown of stars through which higher spirit-wisdom poured into her. She herself was suffused and enveloped by the rays of Sun-forces that had as their source a child who, within her, was about to be born. The dragon's battle is directed against the child of the Sun. He would devour the child when it is born. Michael engages all his spirit-forces to fight this intention. He wishes to help bring to birth the child of the Sun in the woman, the Sun-born ego in humanity's purified soul and subsequently in every single human soul. He casts the dragon down to earth. This apocalyptic spirit-image reveals the activity of world-guidance, the working of Christ for humanity. It encompasses the whole of earth-evolution. The battle for the ego's birth in the human soul against the increasingly powerful Ahrimanic dragon-force is fiercely fought on earth.

The Christ descended to earth during the Fourth Post-Atlantean Epoch, the Greco-Roman Cultural Period. This event was prepared during the 4th century B.C. through Michael's rulership of time. By means of His sacrificial deed on Golgotha, Christ united Himself with the *earth*. From within, the earth began to shine. Her Sun-evolution began. The Sun-seed that Christ planted in the earth started to germinate and grow. Gradually, it illuminated even the deep recesses of humanity. What can come to birth as the ego in our time began to germinate in human souls. What radiated prior to Golgotha from outside, from the Sun, could now ray forth within the inner being of humanity. The spirit-essence of the Sun itself lights up as the core of earth-evolution. The cosmic spirit-image of the woman with the child of the Sun appears behind the Christmas-picture, the birth of the Christ-child through Mary.

From this turning-point in time onward, the anti-Christian Ahrimanic forces have stronger access to humanity's evolution. It means that they acquire greater influence on all human beings who do not wish to unite with the Christ-impulse on earth and thus bypass the Mystery of Golgotha. All those, on the other hand, who do accept the Christ-impulse into themselves, acquire the strength to free themselves from the downward-moving forces:

> From what was said, you can see that through the Christ's appearance, to use this expression, Ahriman was placed in chains, but only for those who try increasingly to grasp and penetrate the Christ-mys-

tery. Less and less can protection against Ahriman's influence be found in the world without the forces streaming from the Christ-mystery.[25]

This is why the Ahrimanic powers work, above all, to conceal the deeper cosmic significance of the Golgotha-event for human beings. But now, with the onset of the time-rulership of the Archangel Michael in the year 1879, an age begins in which a birth "in the spirit" is supposed to occur. What is meant by this? Coming from the heart, the Christ-force now needs to penetrate man's power of cognition. This is so that we can ascend through a transformed thinking to spirit-knowledge and from it unfold the spirit-vision of the future. Conscious recognition of the spirit, conscious spirit-beholding are the fruits of the new event in our time. Christ can now be born as the Sun-ego in our *thinking*. He can overcome the Moon-forces in thinking so that new spirit-cognition can stream in. Once again, the image of the woman with the Sun-child rays forth. Michael works actively on the transformation of hereditary, brain-bound thinking into the Christ-imbued thinking. Those who find the power of thought in thinking, and in the power of thought the actively working "I", experience the first real encounter with their higher "I", the spirit-birth of the "I" in the consciousness soul.[26]

The Fallen Ahrimanic Beings

Perhaps we can gain a better understanding of the battle that was waged on earth between the forces of Michael and the Ahrimanic beings who had been cast down to earth in 1879, when we know what sort of beings we are dealing with. In the lectures, "Wonders of the World, Ordeals of the Soul, Revelations of the Spirit," Rudolf Steiner refers to two groups of angels who in the Egypto-Chaldean period were leaders of humanity. They were entities who had reached their angelic stage as early as the end of the Moon evolution, but then separated during the Egyptian Cultural Period:

> Truly, a great difference exists between these two classes of angelic beings. A comprehension of this difference is vitally important for the greatest mystery of our human evolution.[27]

The lectures describe how Christ, the loftiest cosmic spirit-being, is the teacher and leader of all hierarchical spirit-entities as well. During the descent of Christ from the world's divine source and origin to earth, events occurred for these spiritual beings that resembled the Event of Golgotha for humans.

During the Egypto-Chaldean Cultural Epoch, such an event took place for the angelic beings. It was made possible for the angels to become receptive to the Christ-activity. Angelic beings, who accepted the Christ-impulse, thus reached a higher stage of their development. Other angelic beings, who had united too closely with the impulses that were directed toward the earth, rejected the Christ-impulse.

The forces that tended toward earth were especially powerful during the third cultural period. As we know, this tendency toward earth is connected with the mummification of bodies in Egypt. Rudolf Steiner says about this:

> Imagine how your soul was guided back after death through the passage-way of the pyramid into higher spheres, but your body was held back as a mummy. This had occult consequences. The soul constantly had to look down, if the mummified body was placed below. Thoughts were thus solidified, ossified, and hardened. Thoughts became chained to the physical world [28]

By means of the physical body's preservation, the deceased was to remain connected with the earth beyond the moment of death. Humanity's evolution aimed at that time toward a stronger connection to earth and its forces. This could be accomplished in two ways. It could be carried out through the work of the angels imbued with the Christ-impulse. This would lead to a proper understanding of the Mystery of Golgotha, an event whereby the Christ wished to unite Himself with the earth in order to place the spirit-seed of a new earth in it. On the other hand, if this tendency toward earth was carried out by the angels that rejected the Christ-impulse, the result would be too strong a connection with the *physical* earth. This brought materialism later-on, by which we are surrounded today.

Presently, we live in a recapitulation of the Third Post-Atlantean Cultural Epoch, but on a higher level. In our age, we therefore experience both kinds of angels again, those imbued and those not imbued with the Christ-impulse. Angelic beings, who were able to imbue themselves with the Christ-impulse, inspire and help humans today as spirit-beings under Michael's leadership. This probably underlies the verse, "Michael Imagination":

> You the bright ether-world beings
> Bear the Christ-word to man,
> Thus appears Michael, the Christ-proclaimer,
> To the long-patient, thirsting souls . . .[29]

The others, the non-Christianized, fallen angels, who bonded too powerfully with physical earth-forces, turn into inspirational sources of an atheistic, intellectual thinking, a purely materialistic observation of nature, an intellectual thinking without any moral impulse. Knowledge of these two angelic groups turns into an important key for understanding our age:

> These two streams are mixed together in our age. Our time can only be comprehended if we know that these two streams of spiritual guidance rule in it.[30]

And Rudolf Steiner specifically stresses: "They are beings from the hierarchy of angels who, since the year 1879, have been working among us. . . ."[31]

Two Aspects of Evil

The ego development, purpose and meaning of earth evolution, is not possible without the contributing efforts by the opposing forces. Yet, again and again, we will be led to earth-flight; again and again, we will succumb too strongly to the physical body and therewith to the earth's forces; again and again, we should direct our vision to Christ, Who gives us the strength to stand up to both forces of opposition.

One can gain a curious impression of the great temptations that beset humanity, particularly in California. In the past century, gold was discovered in the northern part of the state. People from all over America flocked to San Francisco and Sacramento to be on time for the huge gold finds. An Ahrimanic gold-fever took hold of everybody. In gold they saw the power to acquire and enjoy all the world's earthly goods and have others work for them. At the beginning of the 20th century, the great dream-factories of motion pictures came into being in southern California in Hollywood. These dream-factories conjured up an utterly illusionary world on movie-screens for people the world over. The audiences ingested this illusionary world with hungry souls. For a brief time, they could rise above the harsh world of outer events. Indeed a Luciferic flight away from earth, but in Ahrimanic distortion!

No other part of America is intrinsically and geographically as close to the East as California. One of the larger states in the U.S with a strong economy, it is a product of opposites, one that cries out for the strength of balance. But here, in the Western world, Ahriman dominates. Let us try to acquire an objective picture of this Ahrimanic world-power which is anti-Christ.

I can contemplate a crystalline structure with its wonderful forms. I can ask myself what sort of forces gave it its shape. I meditate on the formative forces that could produce the exact geometric patterns, the equilateral triangles, right angles, various pentagons, the wonder of the smooth surfaces, the hexagonal crystals, the still greater miracle of the transparency of matter in the condensed substance. No life is present in crystals as is in plants, no movement as is present in animals. Crystals have rigidified for infinite ages. A spellbound universal power of thinking is revealed in the exact forms, in the transparency. As long as this power of thought is still a form-force in the etheric world and as long as it has not yet been enchanted into a rigidified material world, it can shape an infinite variety of constantly changing forms. But if Ahriman takes hold of this cosmic power of thinking, he slays its life and capacity for change and keeps it prisoner in the calcified, incrusted world of substance. But without this earth, condensed as it is by Ahriman, humanity could not evolve, not gain its present consciousness of self.

If we would imagine that Ahriman's all-rigidifying, deadening power would encroach on the plant kingdom in order, there, to produce rigidity and death as in the inorganic world, it would have an evil effect. In their place, the opposing powers are justified; but when they infringe upon other areas, they must be turned back. Only in the struggle with them, the right direction results, the direction that is willed by the spiritual world. In the West, significant aspects of human evolution are being prepared. We can only recognize this when we make the effort to acquire the most objective, unsentimental attitude in regard to current events, particularly the negative aspects, the activity of Ahriman. What is important, according to Rudolf Steiner, is not only:

> that the adversary powers do not take possession of us, but that we confront the actual powers in the right way. We must not only know how to avoid Lucifer, but must conquer and take over his powers to benefit the progressive advance of humanity's culture. We should not merely avoid Ahriman, but conquer his forces to serve humanity's advance.[32]

If we understand these words rightly, they tell us that we need the forces of Ahriman and Lucifer. We must appropriate them in order to fit them in the right way into evolution so that they do not trespass into areas where they produce destruction, death, and so on. We face the task today of launching a higher stage of development of the consciousness soul by means of spiritualizing the thinking forces. This, the Ahrimanic beings wish to prevent. They try to remain at the first stage of this development. They are so convinced of the value and necessity of further refinement of the intellectual reasoning forces that they want to prevent a spiritualization of the forces of knowledge under all circumstances. But with that, humanity's whole culture would be destroyed by the antisocial, fragmenting power of this thinking. Any upward development would be made impossible.

THE REFLECTION IN AMERICA
OF MICHAEL'S BATTLE ON EARTH

Michael's battle against the dragon up until 1879, which took its course in the supersensible world, found its reflection on earth and at the same time was the germination point of coming events. This includes the fact that Michael wishes in a new way to prepare human beings for the Christ by inaugurating a new science, a science of the spirit.

When Rudolf Steiner spoke of this time, he included America in these occurrences:

> What is important is to give a description so that those who are involved will acquire a feeling for the events of the forties [of the 19th century] in Europe and America. . . .[33]

The events in America at that time were indeed significant. The powerful America we know today did not yet exist at the beginning of that period. During the time prior to the Civil War (1861 to 1865), America was in danger of splitting apart. The differences between the states in the South and the North became more and more pronounced. Eleven southern states tried to go their own way. They tried to leave the Union and establish a confederation of southern states. The southerners were primarily farmers; the northern states were an industrial area. This caused great differences. On the one hand, the question of slavery was involved; on the other, the direction America would follow in the future. After the victory of the northern states, the Union was secure. This created the basis for the United States of America to develop into the mightiest industrial nation on earth. America slowly became decisive for the economic and political configuration of the world. Contemporary American civilization grew out of the fully developed intellect and the never-resting will that frequently outdoes itself. The heart or middle-aspect of man, which had had certain roots in the South due to the closeness to nature, was lost to the extent that outward-expanding forces grew stronger.

And yet, particularly at that time, an important seed was planted for a spiritual life in America. It was above all Ralph Waldo Emerson, who wrote his philosophical reflections during that period. He was born in 1803 in Boston, the son of a minister. In 1828, he also became a clergyman. But soon afterwards, in 1832, he gave up his ministry because the Christianity of his age was too narrow-minded for him. He started to develop his own idealistic-spiritual view of the world. He experienced his breakthrough as an author and poet in the year 1841, when his first larger work was published. In it were contained the philosophical essays that became famous later. For many years, he was the center of a circle of friends who actively pursued the same direction as he. Emerson died in 1882, at the beginning of the Michael Age. The time of his activity spanned particularly those years to which we are referring here.

Above all else, one has to recognize in Emerson's case how he struggled to arrive at clarity concerning the nature of human perception and thinking. He referred to two kinds of thinking, an arithmetic-logical thinking and intuitive thinking. He describes the latter form of thinking as a more will-imbued cognition arising out of depths of soul. Regarding this thinking he states:

All our progress is an unfolding, like the vegetable bud. You have first an instinct, then an opinion, then a knowledge, as the plant has root, bud, and fruit. Trust the instinct to the end, though you can render no reason. It is vain to hurry it. By trusting it to the end, it shall ripen into truth and you shall know why you believe.[34]

Emerson shows himself to be a person who is grounded more in the will. For that reason, more than did many others, he experienced his connection with the spiritual aspect of the world. More obviously than others, he sensed the prevailing presence of a spiritual truth in the soul's depths. This truth is initially dull like a germinating instinct. Then a first light of thought is kindled; instincts turn into opinions until, at last, opinions clear up to knowledge. And he had a right to call this form of cognizing an intuitive one, even though it is far removed from what spiritual science calls "intuition." But even as imagination arises from the transformation of thinking, and inspiration comes about through the changed feeling, so does intuition grow out of the transformed will. Intuition has to do with the forces of will. Emerson said:

When we consider the people who have stimulated and supported us, we will become aware of the superiority of the spontaneous or intuitive principle over the arithmetic or logical one. The first contains hidden within itself the nature of the second.[34]

Often, so he explained, one should allow intuitive thinking to speak within oneself. One should not think intentionally, but become silent within and listen. Then, suddenly, one's state of mind can be illuminated all over by the light of a dawning truth, an idea,—even as invisible light makes an object visible when it falls on it.

We can see that Emerson made a great effort to become conscious of a higher intuitive thinking. Moreover, he contemplated the significance of nominalism and realism. Can we not see in this an obvious reflection of the spirit-battle in the supersensible world, which, in view of contemporary materialistic and intellectual thinking, has the purpose of paving the way for a new thinking?

Herman

Again, in ~~Henry~~ Melville's *Moby Dick*,[35] a clear reflection of Michael's battle with the dragon in our time is presented. Melville described the struggle that Captain Ahab had to engage in against the white whale, the largest sperm whale that had ever been sighted. In an initial battle with this monster, Ahab had lost a leg. Since then he had only one goal, to destroy this whale. The tremendous size of the whale and likewise its color that, unlike other sperm whales, was white, demonstrates that a special whale was referred to as the white whale. The significance of this white whale can be made comprehensible by Diether Lauenstein's book, *Das Geheimnis des Wals*.[36] It is perhaps the most profound book ever written about Melville's novel. Lauenstein showed how all that occurs in this novel reveals spiritual happenings, mystery events, in pictorial form. Lauenstein uncovered something important: Captain Ahab, the leader of the whaling ship, is not the hero of the tale. The hero is Ishmael, lone survivor of the battle and narrator of this drama. Step by step, he penetrates the mystery secrets and participates in the battle of life and death to the bitter end. But in his case, death is not victorious; he lives on with his newly acquired insights and experiences, like a person who is moving toward a spiritual rebirth, a man who undergoes the first stage of an initiation.

Herman Melville lived from August 1, 1819 to September 28, 1891. He undertook a first sea voyage at age 18 to Liverpool. At age 21, he started out as a sailor on a whaling ship for eighteen months; the voyage began in 1841. In 1851, he wrote his book, *Moby Dick*. Up above, the battle of Michael with the dragon was being fought out; down below, in imaginative pictures, Herman Melville described the battle against the giant monster, the white whale, who with its tremendous strength sinks the whaling ship and destroys Captain Ahab with the same weapon he had turned against the whale. Only Ishmael escapes death. It is important to recognize the difference between Ahab's and Ishmael's conception of the white whale. Ahab had a most one-sided picture of it. He wanted revenge for what the whale had done to him. He saw "all the hidden devilishness of life, of ventures and all evil become visibly personified and actually attackable in Moby Dick." Ishmael takes a different position regarding the white whale. He sees yet another side. Here is an important passage from Lauenstein's book:

> But when the sperm whale wants to dive into the depth, as we have heard before, it throws its tail of at least 30 feet vertically into the air and for a moment, trembling, remains thus standing.

Ishmael wants to compare the whale in this position only to "majestic Satan." This is meant to be a reference to the animal's menacing nature. But he goes on:

> When you observe such a spectacle, the mood you are in matters. If you feel like Dante, the devil will appear to you; if you feel like Isaiah, then rather the archangels.

For Ishmael, there are two possibilities of viewing the whale. Once like Dante, then one sees the devil and death; again, like Isaiah, and then one sees Jonah who was swallowed by the whale, but rose from death after three days. Christ told people of His age, who asked Him for signs, that He could give them the sign of Jonah; the sign of the willed death so as to arrive at resurrection. But this is the mystery of initiation. Lauenstein therefore said concerning this aspect of the struggle: "This battle represents the voluntary encounter with death." Ahriman is the lord of death on earth. The task of the West is to seek for a spiritual encounter with the forces of death in order to overcome them through spiritual understanding. Then they can be guided to their true place in world evolution. One can see in the whale the sign of the devil. Again, one can see in it a sign for vanquishing death, for initiation. This is most important. In the West, the battle against death must be waged, but not in the manner of Ahab, but in the way Ishmael fights, who sees both sides of evil. Then, as he did, one can survive and find more and more enlightenment on one's spirit quest.

Walt Whitman also lived in the same era, from 1819 to 1892. He belonged to the circle around Emerson and was esteemed by Emerson and his friend, Henry David Thoreau. Thoreau's work likewise falls in the age of which I speak. Through his book on passive resistance, he has influenced even the present time. Gandhi and Martin Luther King received from Thoreau decisive impulses for their activities in India and America, in the East and West. In the midst of the mechanism of economic and political events and the struggle for purely earthly goods, one discovers oases of spiritual life at the time of the Michael struggle, that are like the sowing of seeds for what is to come.

MICHAELIC ACTIVITY OF ANGELS
AND AHRIMANIC OPPONENTS

As was explained earlier, we deal in our time with two groups of angels, a progressive or advanced segment and one that has remained behind. The advanced angels work in full harmony with the Christ-activities in the present age. They are engaged in the unfolding of higher forces of knowledge in humanity:

> And while those angels or Angeloi of the Egyptian-Chaldean Period, who are imbued with the Christ-impulse, let flow into human evolution forces that guide humanity upward to spiritual life, to spirituality, the other beings, who have rejected the Christ-impulse, seek to bestow on human beings as inspirations everything that we can denote as materialistic culture and science.[37]

These are the two important groups of angels who are active in an inspirational manner today among humans. Lacking any morality and ignoring the free development of the human ego, the one angelic group influences human souls with all its powers. The other group of angels works in accordance with the Michael-stream for the reappearing Christ, while fully respecting and considering the impulse of freedom through which alone the ego of man can come to birth. The division that occurred among the angels during the Egyptian age currently takes place among humans. Now we have to decide whether we want to accompany Christ or not. Without Him, we fall prey to dark forces. The decision we on earth will make, for or against the spiritual-Christian path, is something that wafts upward to the angelic world, and prompts the angels to send down influences in the right or wrong way.

If we wonder what it is that these groups of angels do in this case in a concrete way for human beings, we find an answer in the lecture, "The Work of the Angels in Man's Astral Body?"[38] It describes that imaginative perception beholds that

> . . . these beings from the hierarchy of the Angels— and in a sense every single angel who, in regard to each person, has a task, but moreover particularly by working together—form pictures in the human astral body. Under the direction of the Spirits of Form, they form pictures.

If they were not formed, there would be no future for humanity that would correspond to the intention of the Spirits of Form. We know that the Spirits of Form, the seven Elohim, as a totality make manifest the Christ, through whom works the Logos:

> What the Spirits of Form wish to accomplish with us, by the end of earth-evolution and beyond, must first be developed by them in pictures. Subsequently, out of these pictures, emerges transformed humanity, the reality. And even today, through the angels, the Spirits of Form shape these pictures. The angels form pictures in the human astral body, pictures that can be reached with a thinking that has been developed to the point of clairvoyance.

These pictures in turn produce *impulses for the future* in human beings.

But these creative pictures can only have the proper effect if we recognize them; if we learn, in full consciousness, to penetrate and envision angelic activity in our age. To do that, we need the spiritual thoughts of spiritual science:

> The fact is that we live in the age of the consciousness soul. And in this age of the consciousness soul, the Angeloi do what I have just described in the human astral body. Gradually, people should come to the point of comprehending what I have just narrated.

Through their cooperation, the angels arouse three great impulses in us. In future times, nobody will find happiness any more "if others near him or her are unhappy." The "impulse of uttermost brotherliness, of absolute unity of the human race, of properly understood brotherliness in regard to the social conditions in physical life" must become predominant.

The second impulse that can then mature in the soul is "to see hidden divinity in every human being." Man must be understood as the "image of God," as a microcosm in the macrocosm "in concrete, practical life, not merely in theory." Then, no longer can man be viewed as a higher animal. He/she will appear as an image of the spiritual world. This will cause absolute freedom to hold sway in religion.

The third impulse will be that human beings will acquire the possibility of discovering the ruling, creative spirit in the world and humanity through their further evolved thinking. Through thinking, says Rudolf Steiner in this lecture, the abyss can then be surmounted in order to have actual experiences of the spiritual world. A new spirit-perception will be capable of uncovering the spiritual foundations of events on earth. Rudolf Steiner sums up: "Spiritual science for the spirit, freedom of religion for the soul, brotherliness in the corporeal realm. . . ." This presupposes that people become capable of "seeing how the angels go about preparing the future of humanity."

In this way the angels work on making it possible for human beings to be able to experience the all-important event "that is to intervene powerfully in the future configuration of earth evolution." If human beings were to sleep through "the repetition of the Mystery of Golgotha on the etheric plane," meaning, the reappearance of the etheric Christ, then the pictures that the angels weave into the human astral bodies would have no effect. Then the angels would have to implant them into the etheric body instead of the astral body. This process would remain an unconscious one for us. Instead of conscious, free spirit-impulses, instincts that remain unconscious would take hold of us. This would cause us to enter a quite different stream. Angels would then intervene who circumvent the conscious human mind, and work instead through motivating forces that remain instinctive. They work as do group souls in the animal kingdom. Individual animals do not will, but the group-soul-spirits in the animals' instincts do.

Here, we confront one of the most tragic possibilities of contemporary human evolution. If the pictures that the angels weave into our astral bodies are illuminated with consciousness, they become our own. Through our own human force, they imprint themselves into our etheric bodies, thus bringing about a vitalization of the etheric body. This leads a person to living thinking and eventually to spiritual vision, to awareness of the etherically appearing Christ.

In *Anthroposophical Leading Thoughts*, which deals with Michael's activity, we find a wonderful passage:

It is Michael's mission to bring into our etheric bodies those forces through which the shadow-thoughts once again acquire *life* . Then, souls and spirits of the supersensible world will draw near to enlivened thoughts; liberated human beings will be able to live with them. . . .[39]

On the other hand, when angels who were held back work directly into the etheric body, they solidify it and tie it completely to the physical body. The latter then becomes receptive to hidden effects of the earth's forces of gravity. Instinctive urges arise in a person when angels intervene directly in the etheric body, namely, three urges to which we in the West have to pay special attention. Rudolf Steiner characterizes them in "The Work of the Angels in Man's Astral Body" as follows:

First of all, instinctive insights become effective in human beings, insights that are connected "with the mystery of birth and conception along with the whole sexual life. . . ." This would become dangerous for humanity:

> In humanity's evolution, the following would come about: Certain instincts would emerge in a destructive manner out of the life and nature of sexuality instead of appearing in a useful manner in bright, waking consciousness. These instincts would not only signify aberrations, they would pass over into the social life and there produce certain configurations."[40]

Something would ensue in the blood that would prevent brotherhood in humanity and would reduce man to an egotistical instinct-driven being.

Secondly, "an instinctive knowledge of certain remedies" would come about that would result in a significant advancement of materialistic medicine:

Everything connected with medicine will undergo tremendous advancement, but in a materialistic sense. People will acquire instinctive insights into the remedial quality of certain substances and procedures. This will cause enormous damage, but the damage will be termed useful. . . . Pursuant to selfish motives, people will become capable of producing or preventing illnesses.

Thirdly,

. . . certain forces will become known by means of which it will become possible to unleash tremendous mechanical forces in the world, merely by quite easy inducements, through harmonizing certain vibrations. In this way, people will instinctively become acquainted with a certain mental operation of machines and mechanisms and their essential nature, but all technology will then enter murky waters. But these murky waters will please and serve human egotism extraordinarily well.[41]

Already today, the retarded angels are the actual players in outer life. In his memoirs dealing with the beginning of the Communist revolution in St. Petersburg, Leon Trotsky writes that during the first few days he had to address a crowd in a huge circus. He had carefully prepared his text and began to deliver it. All at once, he felt uplifted by the "spirit of the masses" and imbued with another power. He went on speaking extemporaneously, ignoring his text, and spoke much better and more to the point than he himself could have ever done it. This was on an evening that was decisive. Anyone who lived in Germany during the Hitler years, will recall a remark often made by Hitler. He always stressed that he was acting out of "a sleepwalker's certainty." This implies that he felt himself taken hold of by a "higher" power in dreamlike manner.

What happens to a man when he uses his neither recognized nor purified instincts and urges for his own selfish satisfaction, instead of slowly transforming them into conscious, higher forces? Without applying an inner discipline of transformation on himself, he would gradually fall into the state of an egoless being driven by instincts. Forces that could strengthen consciousness would be allowed to go to ruin. In this way, such a man would open himself to group-soul-beings who would turn him into an instrument for their goals.

What would happen if medical science were to view the human being merely as a physical, earthly creature and would only be concerned with making the physical body strong for earthly goals? What if the spiritual human being with its etheric, astral, and spiritual faculties were not seen at all? Increasingly, the human being would grow together with the physical body, and subhuman earth-forces would gain power over him. As a result the etheric body would harden so much that the human being would remain fettered to earth even after death.

What would happen if, inspired by fallen angel beings, human beings could arrive at an instinctive insight into the law of "harmonic vibrations" without seeing through the spiritual basis of this fact? A technology could arise, and we are on the way to it, in which cosmic and earthly forces could be brought to the point of functioning together in such a way that the human being himself would be tied into this mechanical machinery and would turn into a robot in the economic life. People would be robbed of their future. They would lose the possibility of developing their higher faculties.

Rudolf Steiner expressed these insights more than half a century ago. Today, we can see how these three instincts above all have rapidly expanded in humanity. One who is familiar with the lectures, by Rudolf Steiner, *The Challenge of the Times* will recognize the three occultisms as a parallel to the three instincts. In these lectures, Rudolf Steiner refers to eugenic, hygienic, and mechanistic occultism. Based on a natural disposition, eugenic occultism will develop in the East and extend from Russia to Asia. The Middle is inclined toward hygienic occultism. The inclinations of Western peoples tend toward mechanistic occultism. Eugenic occultism leads to a deeper comprehension of the secrets of birth and conception. People will learn, based on certain starry constellations, how to lead souls to birth: "Eugenic capability refers to lifting human propagation out of mere arbitrariness and coincidence."[42] Based on a form of occult wisdom, people will be able to take this in hand. Today we experience how, from the physical end, people make the greatest efforts to achieve arbitrary arrangements in the regulation and prevention of births by physical means. This only leads to an unleashing of sexual forces.

Hygienic forces of healing that will mature out of a natural propensity in Central Europeans can be developed when people there learn and realize how life takes its course from birth to death in a gradual process of dying, one which resembles their process of illness. We bear in ourselves the healthy, constitutive forces:

> And these healing forces—any occultist knows this—are exactly the same as those that one utilizes for acquiring occult faculties, inasmuch as these forces are transformed into perceptions.[43]

This can be understood, if one learns to assess the relationship of the upbuilding forces active in the process of nutrition—the life forces of growth in the body—with the human will. If the creative, constructive forces of life and growth, which are active in human beings as unconscious will, are transformed into conscious forces of cognition, then one gains access to occult forces of healing. A spiritual medicine can develop out of new insights and faculties.

Mechanistic occultism will develop in the West:

> Through this faculty, . . . certain social forms that are at the basis of industrialization today are supposed to be placed on an entirely different basis.

There are those who know that

> to a large extent, machines, mechanistic configurations, and the like can be put in motion by means of the law of harmonious vibrations; through faculties that are latently present and can be developed in the souls of Western people. You find a slight indication of this in what I linked in my Mystery Dramas to the person of Strader.[44]

When this eventually becomes reality,

> the vibrations produced on earth through machines, these negligible earth-vibrations, will take such a course that what is above earth will resonate and vibrate along with what takes place on earth. Our planetary system with its movements will have to resonate with our earth-system, even as a correspondingly tuned string resonates when another string in the same room is plucked.[45]

There are occult associations in the West that know of these things and promote them; they moreover have knowledge of the possibilities of eugenic occultism in Russia and

Asia and hygienic occultism in Central European countries. They try to acquire these faculties as well, so that they can thereby attain predominance in the world. The right thing would be if the faculties of East, West, and the Middle would be developed and brought to harmonious, free, joint activity, so that a feeling could arise that it is just in the cooperation between East, West, and the Middle that something can develop that would serve and benefit all humanity.

If we bring to mind the greatly differentiated activities of the angels and of those angels who have remained behind, the serious danger threatening humanity in our time is recognized. It is the danger of division, indicated as well in Revelation, which in pictorial manner refers to human beings with the sign of the beast and the sign of God on their foreheads. If we do not see this danger, then we are not awake in the present.

THE ANCIENT MEXICAN
MYSTERIES AND AMERICA

In his lectures, "Inner Impulses of Evolution in Humanity," Rudolf Steiner describes circumstances in the ancient mystery centers of Central America. The most important civilization with its pyramids, temples, other sacred structures, and any number of artifacts was founded by the Mayans. Their civilization existed from about 300 B.C. to the fifteenth century A.D.; then followed its gradual demise. The center of Mayan activity was located in Guatemala and Honduras. It extended even to southern Mexico. The civilization of the Mexican Toltecs began around 200 B.C., spread out in Mexico and lasted until 1224. Then followed the Aztecs. In the days of Christ's life on earth, we are dealing primarily with Mayans and Toltecs. The population had retained very different forces than the Europeans, who at that time already were developing powers of thinking. This population consisted of humble souls, endowed with ancient, primitive, atavistic faculties:

> But among this population, a large number could be found who were initiated into certain mysteries. The greatest variety of mysteries existed in the Western hemisphere, . . . mysteries that had a large following for certain teachings that emerged out of these mysteries.[46]

The lectures contain a description of a being that was worshipped in ancient Atlantis and was called the "Great Spirit." They moreover describe how this being's effects continued on in the Post-Atlantean Epoch. In the book by William H. Prescott, *The World of the Aztecs*, the following is said about it:

> The Aztecs believe in the existence of a highest creator and lord of the universe. They address him in their prayers as "the god through whom we have life." "Omnipresent, he knows all our thoughts, gives us all gifts," "without whom we do not exist," "invisible, not incarnated, a god of greatest perfection and purity."[47]

He was the *one* god who united and bore within himself all other gods, humanity, and the whole of existence. This view of the "Great Spirit" survived the destruction of Atlantis.

There are Mayan, Toltec, and Aztec myths that point to a link between their origin and ancient Atlantis. Today, the assumption is that the indigenous people of America came from Asia across the Bering Straits and Canada to present-day Alaska. The ancient myths trace the origin of the indigenous population directly to Atlantis. In the legends from Central America about the Flood, there is reference to Tezcalipoca who caused the waters to recede after the sinking of Atlantis. Following that, Coxcox or Teppi, the Noah of the Mexicans, could land his ship in America. The book, *Atlantis, the Antediluvian World* by Ignatius Donnelly, in which myths of the Flood from all over the world are collected, likewise contains the legends that existed among the Mayans, Toltecs, and Aztecs. In this book, the following is related concerning the great migrations, of which sagas have survived to this day:

> Bancoff reports that the Toltecs trace their migration-route back to their point of departure that was called Azylan or Atlan. The Aztecs likewise appear to have come from Aztlan. The name Aztecs was derived from Aztlan. They were Atlanteans.[48]

Along with them, the notion of the "Great Spirit" moved westward. Two streams of this view of the "Great Spirit" came about. One stream, on the world's eastern half, assumed a more Luciferic character, the other stream on the western half, an Ahrimanic quality. The concept of the "Great Spirit" continued in America throughout the Post-Atlantean Epoch until the discovery of America and down through all the Indian tribes even to the Indian descendants of the present. An Indian chief, born in 1870, recorded his memories in a book, *The Memoirs of Chief Red Fox.* One chapter deals with the "Great Spirit." This is how it begins:

> Among American Indians, only one religious view existed, independent of the tribe and geographic locations. They believed that the finite and infinite are expressions of the one, universal, absolute being who defines the outlines for morality and leadership among them and who produces every living being. They named this being the "Great Spirit."

In the mystery centers of the West, above all in Central America, a descendant of the "Great Spirit" was revered:

> Like a unified power, obeyed and followed by all, a ghostly spirit was worshipped. This spirit was a descendant of the "Great Spirit" of Atlantis. It was a spirit, however, that gradually had assumed an Ahrimanic character, inasmuch as it tried to work with all those forces that were appropriate in Atlantis, but even there had become Ahrimanic.[49]

Rudolf Steiner describes further how this scion of the "Great Spirit" of Atlantis bore a name that resembles the Chinese word Tao. This offspring of the "Great Spirit" in the West had a name that was like a caricature of the name "Tao," namely, "Taotl." "It was an Ahrimanic degeneration of the "Great Spirit," a powerful being, but one that did not come to physical incarnation."[50]

What kind of forces were these that were justified in ancient Atlantis, but no longer so in the age of the Western mysteries? They were the forces that brought greater density to both the earth, which in Atlantean times had not yet solidified quite so much, and to human beings who still had softer, more pliable bodies. Since the middle of the Atlantean age, when the dragon forces had been cast down to earth, these forces exerted an ever growing effect. They were nurtured in the mysteries:

> Many were initiated into the mysteries of Taotl. But the initiation was certainly one that bore an Ahrimanic character, for it had a quite definite purpose and goal. Its goal was to rigidify, to mechanize all earthly life, even that of human beings, to the greatest extent possible. We could say that an earthly kingdom of death was envisioned, one that was directed from within toward smothering all independence, any stirring of the soul. In the mysteries of Taotl, forces were supposed to be acquired that would enable human beings to create a completely mechanized civilization on earth.[51]

The term, "mechanized," when used by Rudolf Steiner, refers to two things. He states that the attempt is made from this side

> not only to establish a culture that would have culminated in nothing but mechanical instruments, but would have turned human beings into mere robots.[52]

He referred here mainly to ego-less human beings who in all their actions are directed only from outside. In order to establish such a mechanized earthly kingdom, the priests of these mysteries had to obtain unusual faculties, faculties that would enable them to rule over and make use of the forces of hardening, mechanization, and death on earth. They had to be initiated in a very specific black-magical manner and had to acquire the mysteries of death in such a way that they were able to become masters over the death-forces. To this end, the priests of these temple centers perpetrated ritual murders.

It is a known historical fact that the practice of ritual sacrifice existed in ancient times in many temple sites of Central America, where people were killed by the priests. To their horror, the Europeans, who arrived with Cortez in Mexico, still witnessed these murders that were carried out by priests. Certain sensations were to be evoked by means of these murders, particularly in the mysteries of Taotl, that could turn the priests to masters of the death forces in the world. The slayings in which a priest killed the victim by cutting the heart out of the chest are known in history. Even today we can see illustrations of such ritual murder on stone tablets. The victim is lying, for instance, on a sacrificial stone slab. Four assistants are holding him down; his chest is open. The priest lifts the heart up to the sun with his right hand. Rudolf Steiner speaks of stomachs having been cut out of victims. Historically, this is probably unknown. Such a contradiction might pose a riddle, but a solution may be found, if we pay heed to what Rudolf Steiner described. He said that the mysteries of Taotl, in which these sacrifices occurred, were carried out in strictest secrecy without any knowledge by the outer world. It makes sense that in these mysteries the invasive procedure did not take place in the human rhythmic system but in that of metabolism, digestion, and will. For the intention was to penetrate into the will sphere, the core of Western humanity, in order to turn human beings into instruments.

The lectures quoted here furthermore outline that, aside from these horrible mysteries, others existed too that tried to take a stand against this cruel human slaughter. Around the time of the Mystery of Golgotha, a new movement formed in Mexico. With resolute earnestness, its members committed to opposition against the Ahrimanic mystery centers. From this movement emerged a lofty initiate whom Rudolf Steiner calls Vitzliputzli. Here, we come to one of the most remarkable reports by spiritual science, one of greatest significance for America. Even the description of this exalted initiate attests to his greatness and importance:

> At a certain moment in time, the following came to pass: A being was born that set itself a task within this culture, a being that was born in today's Central America. The Mexicans, the ancient indigenous inhabitants of Mexico, had a certain perception concerning the existence of this being. They said that this being came into the world, because a virgin had begotten him as her son, a virgin who had immaculately conceived him through supersensible powers. A feathered being had been the impregnator of this virgin, a feathered being that had come from heaven. If one pursues these matters by the occult means at one's disposal, one discovers that this being, to whom the ancient Mexicans ascribe a virgin-birth, reached the approximate age of 33; this being was furthermore born around the year 1 of our calendar.[53]

It is quite remarkable to realize that in the same year when a virginal birth occurred in Palestine, a virginal birth took place in America as well, namely, the birth of a great initiate, and that this initiate reached the same age as Christ

Jesus. At age 33, he withdrew once more into the spiritual world. These are surprising parallels!

> In Vitzliputzli, these people revered a Sun-being who was born of a virgin . . . concerning whom one finds . . . that he was the unknown contemporary of the Mystery of Golgotha in the Western hemisphere.[54]

At the time of the Mystery of Golgotha, all those who belonged with Michael were united on the Sun. From the Sun came this lofty initiate who had chosen for himself a certain task in America.

At the same time, one of the greatest black magicians had emerged from the above-described Ahrimanic mysteries, who had prepared himself through many incarnations and murders.

> He was one of the greatest, if not the very greatest, black magicians who has ever walked the earth, a black magician who, therefore, had appropriated for himself the greatest secrets that can be acquired on this path. He was about to face a significant decision when the year 30 approached. It was the decision actually to become so powerful by means of the ongoing initiation as a single human individuality that he would have known a fundamental secret. This secret would have enabled him to give subsequent human earth evolution an impetus that would have darkened humanity of the Fourth and Fifth Post-Atlantean Periods to the point where goals that the Ahrimanic powers were envisioning would have been realized.[55]

If the black magician had been successful in what he had intended during the time of the Mystery of Golgotha, not only the Fourth Post-Atlantean Epoch but also the Fifth, hence our epoch, would have been filled with darkness. It would have signified that the spiritual breakthrough we experience in Anthroposophy today could not have taken place, but that the intentions of the Ahrimanic beings would have succeeded. This is how the events that occur in the Western hemisphere connect with Central Europe and the whole world.

As was said, the greatest black magician who ever walked the earth lived in those days in the West. The Apocalypse likewise knows of such an all-powerful magician. He is the "false prophet," who is in the service of the beast, which in turn is the actual anti-Christian adversary. At the end of earth-evolution, the beast and the false prophet are overcome:

> And the beast was captured, and with it the false prophet who in its presence had worked the signs by which he deceived those who had received the mark of the beast and those who worshipped its image.[56]

Have we come across an earthly trace of him here in Central America?

What happens on one continent, even if that continent is far away, has significance for the whole of humanity. This can become especially clear to us when we visualize the mighty, decisive battle which the great initiate of the Sun had to wage against this black magician. It lasted three years, namely from 30 to 33 A.D. This is exactly the time from the Baptism in the Jordan to the Event on Golgotha, meaning precisely the length of time that the Christ-being spent on earth. When Christ overcame death on Golgotha, the Sun-initiate, of whom Rudolf Steiner says that he was a Sun-being in human form, succeeded in overcoming the black magician and to nail him on a cross. This disabled the power of this magician and therewith Ahriman's power.

Is there a parallel in the Deed of Christ on Golgotha that corresponds to this event in Mexico? In the first of the two lectures, *The Deed of Christ and the Opposing Spiritual Powers,* we read:

> It is more than merely a pictorial manner of speech that, following the Event on Golgotha, at the moment when the blood flowed from the wounds on Golgotha, the Christ appeared in the netherworld, the realm of shades, and placed Ahriman in chains. Even though Ahriman's influence remained—and basically all of humanity's materialistic ways of thinking must be traced back to him—and although this influence can only be paralyzed if human beings comprehend and accept the Event of Golgotha, yet, this Event has become *the* source from which we can attain the strength once again to come into the spiritual divine world.[57]

The overthrow of the Ahrimanic initiate takes place in concurrence with the Christ-event in Palestine. One can imagine that the forces which were developed through Christ during the three years on earth flowed across to the Sun-initiate, who as one who was initiated beheld the events of Golgotha with his inner eye so as to keep his deed in accordance with Him. This gave rise to the forces that enabled him to defeat the black magician. And this in turn prevented the darkness, that would have emanated from the victory of the black magician, from gripping Europe. Ahriman's effects were largely subdued and to the extent that they were still effective in America, they were held back. In this way the Fourth Cultural Epoch could unfold correctly and likewise the beginning of the Fifth. Ahriman was assigned the place where he

is allowed to be active, namely, in the interior of the earth and the inorganic world.

What is so amazing about this event in America? The fact that despite the Mystery of Golgotha such a conquest of the Ahrimanic power in America was still necessary! Why did such an event have to take place in the West? Was the Christ-deed in Palestine not enough? This riddle must be carefully approached. But something else is equally important and perhaps even more significant than the defeat of the black magician. And this is that the Sun-initiate could implant the Christ-forces directly into the American continent through his victory over the magician.

We may come a little closer to a solution to this puzzling question, if we call to mind that, in the West, the Ahrimanic elemental powers rise out of the interior of the earth. They do so more strongly than in any other part of the world. In order to understand this, we must become aware of an important fact that is connected with the activity of Ahrimanic powers. Not only once, but several times Rudolf Steiner makes use of a picture in these lectures. He says that comprehension of this picture only dawns gradually when one meditates on it for some time. He says concerning people of today:

> Modern human beings only have weak reflexes. . . in their soul . . . of what rushes and surges in their subsensory nature and at most comes up like ghostly shivers in frightening dream images, yet even then only in a weak way. Modern man does not know what happens there.[58]

And in order to explain what takes place in a person's subsensory nature, he makes use of the following picture:

What modern man experiences in his soul could be compared with what you experience when standing on completely volcanic ground. It can be quite tranquil at first. But you need only take a piece of paper and light it, and smoke billows up everywhere. And if you could see in the smoke what is boiling and surging below, you would know what kind of ground you are really standing upon.[59]

In the Apocalypse the two-horned beast, the actual anti-Christian power, also rises up out of the *earth*. But how could it become so powerful in the West? The horrible Ahrimanic mysteries have to do with this. Maybe there would have been no deliverance from the onslaught of the Ahrimanic powers without the deed on the part of the Sun-initiate. This in turn leads to the question of what the task is that the West has to carry out for the whole of humanity. If this task is not clearly and fully understood, one merely forges a shadow-sword that cannot accomplish anything in reality against the tremendous unfolding of Ahriman's power in this part of the world.

In the above-mentioned lectures, reference is made to an onslaught of Ahrimanic forces against the then existing Roman empire. In so doing, these forces made the attempt to develop a completely mechanized state system. People and nations were to be incorporated into this system in such a way that they would only have been cogs in a huge state-mechanism.

The Ahrimanic forces counted on a certain rigidity that would come about on earth through Romanism, a rigidity expressed in blind obedience and subjugation under Romanism.[60]

A state was supposed to come about.

That was to include in its structure all human activities, a state that could have been directed from Rome with strictest centralism and the worst expansion of power. . . . [61]

It is important to detect this centralizing effort on the part of the Ahrimanic powers on earth, because, as Rudolf Steiner explained, following the destruction of the Roman empire, Rome's spirit works on in ghostlike form and tries to realize in the world what it failed to accomplish in Rome. It will try to do this again and again. It strives to incarnate again. Could we not observe this in the two World Wars ? Were there not nations with such aims, nations that believed they could establish a Roman empire, a world empire so as to subjugate the world under their rule? These attempts will continue with more and more concentrated effort. In Rome, the Ahrimanic powers could not attain their goal, because the natural egoism of the Romans resisted it, and because the barbarian invasions broke up all established forms. Rudolf Steiner sums up what he said about the Roman empire in the following way:

Now, Roman history is by no means a manifestation of Ahrimanic powers. I ask you specifically to pay attention to this. These powers stand in the background and Roman history is a battle against the Ahrimanic forces.[62]

This is likewise true of the West. Rudolf Steiner had this to say about the significance of the discovery or rediscovery of America. It had been preceded by the Mongolian offensive into Europe. In Asia as well, a descendant of the "Great Spirit" of Atlantis was active, but he had assumed Luciferic traits. He was served there by a powerful, initiated priest.

This priest chose Ghengis Khan as his instrument. Subsequently, during their campaign that devastated everything, the Mongolians moved through Russia into Central Europe. They overran any resistance that stood in their way. They came as far as Liegnitz and were victorious there, too. But then the strange thing happened that they began to withdraw after their victory. Yet, even though the Mongolians withdrew somewhat, the Luciferic "Great Spirit" with its Luciferic images and forces could penetrate into and infest the Occident.

The discovery of America was brought about by world-guidance in order to create an earthly counterbalance against this mighty Luciferic temptation in the Occident. Through this development, a beneficial counterweight became effective, a trend directed toward the earth. Through the working-together of both these streams, there arose in Central Europe what was supposed to develop in the middle. In regard to America, Rudolf Steiner added:

> I do ask you not to tell others that I depicted the discovery of America as an Ahrimanic deed; I stated the opposite. I said that America had to be discovered, had to be found, and that all this was necessary in the progressive course of world development. I only pointed out that Ahrimanic powers interfered in this, interferences that are onslaughts against what is supposed to take place in the progressive course of world evolution.[63]

If we now turn our attention to America, we must distinguish between America's significance in the spiritual world-configuration, and the Ahrimanic beings who rage against this. We must therefore say of America what Rudolf Steiner said of Rome: The history of America, the western half of the earth, "is by no means a manifestation of Ahrimanic powers. I ask you specifically to pay attention to this. These powers stand in the background," and American history, "is a battle against the Ahrimanic forces." Here, Ahriman did not only establish his main center of activity; here, moreover, the victory of a great Sun-initiate over the Ahrimanic forces took place. On this continent, not only are Ahrimanic forces effective, but likewise the death-defying resurrection-forces of the Mystery of Golgotha. But with this, the power of Ahriman is not broken. It is due to him that the Golgotha-event passed many human beings by without a trace. He tries again and again, and with ever greater effort to attain his goal. In our age we confront his greatest and most decisive assault. In the age when Christ suffers death of consciousness in the etheric world, a death which will lead in growing measure to the light-filled resurrection of Christ in the consciousness of human beings, the Ahrimanic adversary forces are gathering strength to strike their most powerful blow. In our age, the decision will be made whether humanity's evolution can be continued in the spirit of the Mystery of Golgotha, or whether Ahriman will turn it into his direction. The center from which this counterblow will proceed is located in America. The Ahrimanic powers have prepared the ground for this, long since. But it is not their intention to limit their activity to the West. They wish to make it effective all over the world and especially in Central Europe where the portal to a new spirit-perception was opened.

If the action of *one* man, even if he was a black-magical initiate and Ahriman's power backed him up, was able to have the consequences described above, then we cannot discount the fact that the effects will be much greater and more powerful when Ahriman himself can lead the attack on earth. Since the 15th century, Ahriman is preparing his coming in America.

This is the reason why much can be done here to become aware of the intention of the Ahrimanic beings and how they go about realizing their aims. Becoming aware of this is not only a matter of thinking, it is the most important thing we can do in our age. Should we not assume that the Sun-initiate, who was victorious over the black magician in Mexico, views the struggle for acquiring such awareness with supportive concern and deep earnestness? The following words by Rudolf Steiner demonstrate what humanity is facing:

> In the coming age, the spiritual beings, who are called Asuras, will surreptitiously creep into the consciousness soul and, with that, into what is termed the human ego—for the ego imbues the consciousness soul. The Asuras will develop evil with a much more intense force than even the Satanic powers of the Atlantean or the Luciferic spirits of the Lemurian age.[64]

At the turning point of time, the spiritual world sent the initiate, who came from the Sun, to the West to divert the threatening consequences of the Ahrimanic mysteries as far as this was possible. In the Roman empire, human beings instinctively and unconsciously prevented the rise of a state-mechanism in which people and nations would have been will-devoid cogs in the state's machinery. In our age, the age of the consciousness soul, human beings must cooperate in full consciousness. Rudolf Steiner said:

> Since the middle of the 15th century, we live in an age where humanity should come increasingly into possession of the full force of consciousness. As the incarnation of Ahriman approaches, the important thing for human beings is to face this event in full consciousness. When the incarnation of Lucifer took

place, it was actually perceptible only to the prophetic faculty of the priests in the mysteries. What the Christ-incarnation represented through the Event on Golgotha likewise eluded much of human awareness. But humanity must consciously go and meet the incarnation of Ahriman amid the upheavals that will occur on the physical plane. . . . One of our tasks for the impending development of civilization will be to confront Ahriman's incarnation with such clear awareness that this incarnation can actually serve humanity to advance toward a higher spiritual development.[65]

Just seeing and anticipating such a possibility signifies unceasing encouragement for any spiritually aspiring person. The incarnation of Ahriman cannot be prevented, but by becoming fully aware of the facts connected with Ahriman's incarnation and the etheric Coming of the Christ in our time, we can do something most decisive. The direction that matters will take in the next century will depend, to a large degree, on human beings. By struggling to gain an ever clearer consciousness, we can summon the Christ-imbued Michaelic angels to our side.

Mechanistic Occultism and Professions

It has been pointed out that mechanical or mechanistic occultism will develop in the West. We must call to mind that the West is dealing above all with economic developments. Rudolf Steiner mentions that humanity's life in recent times can only be comprehended, if the division into a Western economical element, a political-governmental-legal element in Middle Europe, and a religious element in the East is understood.

I saw a eurythmy performance in which Rudolf Steiner's "Twelve Moods" of the Zodiac were presented where the sun moved together with the planets through the whole circle— from constellation to constellation. Each constellation, each planet had its own gestures and movements that had been brought down from heaven, as it were. The cosmic movements of the starry world could swing into these gestures. There were moments when I felt: What is present here are not only human, subjective movements by the eurythmists, but cosmic-objective ones that swing and weave into them. The aforementioned "law of harmonic vibrations," that is utilized by mechanistic occultism, works in the opposite direction, but can be understood better through such an experience.

Aside from the forces of electricity, magnetism, gravity, and atomic fission, the law of harmonic vibrations will come into play in the future. Rudolf Steiner speaks of two possibilities: of a form of mechanistic occultism that is destructive to mankind, and one that will serve humanity. In reference to machines that produce destructive effects, he says:

If you observe certain segments of what is effective presently, you will realize that part of our contemporary civilization is well on its way to pursue this horrible element of decline.[66]

Anything that people do on earth, any new inventions, are seeds for the future. They grow and mature, along with the rest of evolution, to their eventual actual significance. So, too, it is with professional life, with what is created through vocations. It will go on developing on earth and continue on Jupiter, on Venus, and on the Vulcan condition of Earth. Only then will the meaning of this germinal beginning become evident. Naturally, the physical products that were created, machines, factory-complexes, in short, everything that came into being, will vanish. Initially, they become independent of man:

> Particularly through all the intensifications that will occur, what humanity achieves in professional activities will, at the same time, detach itself from the human being, and become more objective. Due to this, in further developments during the Jupiter, Venus, and Vulcan evolutions, human accomplishments will pass through something similar to what was attained for Earth through Old Saturn, Sun, and Moon, specifically through this process of detachment.[67]

The term "detachment" has threefold meaning here. All the external products created in economic life become detached from the human being. But along with this, interest in the work to be done becomes detached which, in reality, has been true for a long time. People no longer pursue their work with the same enthusiasm and interest that imbued them once upon a time. The inner bond with a given profession increasingly vanishes. A certain necessity arises therefore "to develop conditions that have cosmic significance, especially because professional life is becoming detached in a certain sense from human interests."[68] For, due to the fact that the more subjective, personal relationship to work is gone, something quite different can enter into work, something objective.

A long time ago, friends and I were on a bio-dynamically run farm. The owner of the farm showed us a small square plot of land divided into four equal parts. Four different people had sown wheat—each on one square. The soil was the same on all four, it had been worked the same way, the weather conditions were identical. All four took their seeds from the same sack of wheat. Only the four human beings differed from each other. And the half-grown plants on the field's four sections were just as different. On one, they had grown quite tall. On another, they were still small; on yet another, growth seemed stunted and of delicate shape. On one, the plants were strong and healthy. It made quite an impression when the farmer said: "For once, I wanted to determine a person's influence on a plant." Something flows from a person into plants. Rudolf Steiner stated in the above-mentioned lecture:

> The delicate pulsations inherent in a person's life of will and attitude will increasingly blend with, and fit into what a man produces. It will not be a matter of indifference whether you receive a prepared substance from one person or another.[69]

Something becomes detached from the human will-life, when emotions are silenced. This then unites with the products created by a person. The forces of exalted spiritual beings are effective in human will, for example, the Thrones, the Spirits of Will. On Ancient Saturn, they gave up their will-substance so that corporealities could gradually come into being. In the lecture mentioned above it says:

> In what we create in our line of work, through manual or so-called white-collar labor, lies the source of incorporation, so to speak, of spiritual beings. At this time in the earth's evolution, these spiritual beings are as yet of an elemental nature . . . of the fourth degree.[70]

Our physical and mental activity actually flows into agricultural and industrial products and confers on them a spiritual existence, even when the material products cease to exist. Indeed, an invisible, spiritual-cosmic occurrence is linked with the economic and vocational life. This gives us a completely new perspective on all that takes place in professions and the economy, and likewise on what is developing in the West.

Something else is connected with all these processes:

> To the same degree that the products of human labor will no longer be generated with special enthusiasm, all that thus flows out of human beings can . . . turn into motor power, because that is a necessary condition.[71]

Here we stand at the cradle of mechanistic occultism. The astonishing thing is that the mighty, invisibly working, cosmic relationships, that cooperate with humanity's economic and professional life, have something to do with the origin of a motor or kinetic force, one that springs from the spiritual will element of the human being and has something to do with mechanistic occultism:

One, who can have even a slight idea of the future of technological developments, knows that in time to come, depending on who runs a plant, whole factories will have individual effects. Human attitude will enter into the factory and be transferred to the ways and means in which the machines operate. The human being will grow together with objectivity. Everything that we will touch in the future will by degrees bear an imprint of our being.[72]

Through the vibrations of certain signs "motion is produced in a motor which is calibrated for this sign."[73] If we consider the implications of these statements by Rudolf Steiner, we understand that spirit-aware people must first produce the kinetic energy before it can become effective on earth. Strader, who appears in Rudolf Steiner's Mystery Dramas, may well have created a properly functioning model, yet it would not immediately become functional, because the vibrations of the sign would still be missing.

Strongly developed *moral* power is required for this, something Rudolf Steiner describes as follows:

Picture a truly good person in the future, one who really possesses a high nobleness of mind. Such a person will be able to construct machines and devise signs for them that can only be executed by people who have the same attitude of mind as he, meaning, who are likewise of noble mind and heart.[74]

Rudolf Steiner obviously describes a form of mechanistic occultism here that will emerge through a spiritual advancement shared by like-minded persons. In such an event, if the cosmos, the world of the stars, takes part in these vibrations, then it happens based on a correctly beheld cosmos, meaning, a spiritually beheld cosmos. But there also exists an

Ahrimanic possibility to put mechanistic occultism into practice. We have heard that elemental beings incorporate into the will-impulses that flow from human beings into the work they do:

> But it is important . . . that they come into being in the *right* way, not only that they come into being in general. Elemental spirits that disturb as well as serve the world-process can thus be generated.[75]

When the angels who did not take up the Christ-impulse develop the creative images not in the human astral body, in which case that person can remain free, but, by passing consciousness, in the etheric body, then the will is seized by Ahriman. The will-impulses then are of a different kind, are Ahrimanically destructive.

When a person, who undergoes an inner development based on the Spirit of the Middle, wants to develop his occult predispositions, he may not do so based on any hatred or forces of antipathy:

> On the other hand, the predisposition to a later occult faculty is in a sense supported when it is developed out of certain instincts of hatred. It is a strange phenomenon.[76]

This phenomenon points to something important. Criticism, antipathy, and hatred arise in human beings when abstract antisocial thinking reaches from the head down to the will-sphere. The will is then not redeemed by spirit-knowledge but is taken hold of directly by such head-thinking. Destructive forces are thus engendered in which Ahriman is effective. Then, associations are developed to electricity, to the magnetism of the earth, and to the destructive power of atomic fission.

Eventually, machines have to come into existence that embody not only intelligence and energy, but by virtue of the law of harmonious vibrations represent the human rhythmic system as well. Only this system can unite intelligence and energy, thinking and willing in a *constructive rhythm.* This rhythm will not manifest through a circular movement, the way we picture the planets circling around the sun today. It will manifest through the rhythm of the middle-part of man, where the blood circulates in the form of a lemniscate that connects above and below crosswise. The above can only come to pass when self-interest and egotism no longer dominate industry; when struggles of competition and wages no longer destroy cooperation, and the economy acquires deeper meaning. Then the economic sphere can take its proper place by the side of a cultural life that can only develop in freedom, and a democratic life of the state that keeps watch over its people's equality in the life of rights. Tendencies toward such a threefold society can be detected during the establishment of the United States of America more than 200 years ago. Today, however, they are quite obscured.

The help that should be offered the West is to view what goes on in America in a spiritual light. There have to be those who can see the economic life, seemingly the most materialistic structure in the world, in its cosmic and spiritual significance.

The double in the human being opposes the development of a spiritualized America. Without an understanding of the double's activity in the West, one easily falls victim to illusions concerning what is possible, or turns bitter due to inescapable disappointments. If one learns to know this double, one gains a profound comprehension of what truly takes place in the West.

We see the emergence of a serious task in the Western hemisphere. An attempt should be made to acquire an awareness, through inner work, about what is being prepared here, on the one hand from the Ahrimanic side, but then also from the Christian spiritual side. Up to now, we sense this task only dimly, a task that is supposed to be fulfilled in the mighty conflict that has broken out concerning the future of the earth and humanity. It must yet confront us more clearly. Growing awareness of it is the weapon that can lead ongoing developments in positive directions. To this, the second part of these studies is dedicated.

PART II

INTRODUCTION

Looking back over the first part, we recall that one concern was to demonstrate that we can speak not only of the three-fold configuration of the human being or the threefold social organism, but, as did Rudolf Steiner at the East-West Congress in Vienna, of a threefold world-situation of East, West, and Middle. As different as the metabolic and limb system is from the rhythmic system or the head-and-nerves system, and as different as the economic life in the social organism is from the life of rights, of law, or the spiritual-cultural life, so the West differs from both the East or the European Middle, when we look at the inner predispositions. Rudolf Steiner always tried to make it clear that each one of the three domains would have to develop out of its *own* capacities. For only then would the results truly benefit all humanity.

In the Western part of the world, people live primarily in the metabolic and limb system that contains the unconscious will. Will is the active force in all nutritive processes, the force of motion in our limbs, the force in our instincts and urges. But if we penetrate further with spiritual perception into the inner nature of the will force, it manifests as a power rooted in the higher spiritual world, a power that keeps the human being in constant connection with the cosmos and its universal activity. This higher sphere of the spirit world is only accessible to intuition. It is the sphere where humans dwell in deep sleep or after death, united with all beings and processes. In this sphere, the will is pure sacrificial will.

Presently, in waking day-consciousness, will is asleep and its effects remain completely in the unconscious.

Now, the will can be awakened when the light of spiritual wisdom enters its dark realms. This can be likened to the gradual awakening of a cosmic human being who is otherwise asleep in us. In this way, we learn to recognize how our spiritualized will can stream upwards through the rhythmic human nature, the heart, into intellectual thinking; how such a will is then capable of transforming this thinking and filling it with life. In turn, thinking is then able to understand all processes of nature and the world more deeply. The stream of life-awakening light of knowledge can once more flow down through the heart into the will. There, it can arouse its deeper predispositions, namely, the impulse of brotherhood that unites all human beings and the life-creating substance of sacrifice. Such a will can work even into the hardest of earth's elements so as to transform them into something spiritual. One who engages in these efforts will realize how the human nature of the middle, the heart, was crushed in Western civilization between intellectual thinking and instinctive will and thus robbed of its creative power. We then recognize how, due to this, all humane elements vanished in our time; how chaotic, wild forces of destruction were unleashed which, nowadays, we see springing up so rapidly. On the other hand, if the heart is pervaded once more by the spiritualized forces flowing up and down, it is spiritualized and etherized, and thus regains its creative power.

In this way, based on our own experience, we learn to recognize and know not only the West (will) in ourselves, but likewise the Middle (heart, feeling) and the East (spirit). Experiencing the West, Middle, and East in ourselves signifies becoming world-citizens. Vladimir Soloviev once referred to this truth in the following words:

In this sense, we can say that human society is the complement or extension of the personality. The personality, on the other hand, is the concentrated content of society.[77]

One thing more must then be done. We must thoroughly become acquainted with the powers who are antagonistic to such a development. We can resist them only through penetrating recognition of their nature and opposing activities. Then, we can even change some of their aspects into a good, positive direction.

THE DANGER OF THE
DOUBLE FOR WESTERN MAN

Rudolf Steiner's descriptions of the double, the Doppelgänger
of the human being, are most significant. And they are of special importance for the West. Shortly before their re-entry
into earthly life, all human beings are invaded by a being that
accompanies them throughout their lives, but leaves them
again shortly before death. In the lecture, "The Secret of the
Doppelgänger," the following is stated concerning this being:

> The way the human body develops, these beings
> can, as it were, enter this body at a certain moment
> prior to birth. Then they accompany us below the
> threshold of consciousness. There is only one thing
> about the human body they absolutely cannot tolerate,
> and that is death. This is why they always have to
> abandon the human body in which they have settled
> before it falls victim to death. Again and again, it is a
> bitter disappointment to these beings, for the very
> goal they wish to attain is to remain in human bodies
> beyond death. This would be a great achievement in
> these beings' domain. As yet, they have not arrived at
> this point.[78]

They unite with the unconscious part of the human body,
the part that we cannot penetrate with present-day consciousness. Human beings, who in reality are spiritual beings
and whose home is the spiritual world, need assistance when
they try to incarnate and live in a realm that in all regards is
the opposite of their original home, a realm where darkness,

disease, and death rule. The double ties us to the earth and hardens our thinking, feeling, and will. The influence of the supersensible world is subdued and we become receptive to our tasks on earth. This is the true purpose of the double. In the present, however, this double is completely permeated by Ahriman and has the tendency to link a person with the earth's lower forces, to compress the body and place lower human nature into its service.

A number of questions arise here: Does the double unite with the body's material substance or with its invisible form, the form that was corrupted by Lucifer and then restored and developed further by Christ? Does the double wish to acquire this corrupted body in order, eventually, to pass across death's threshold with it? Why does it, at present, have to depart from the body shortly before death? And why is that a bitter disappointment for it? Many unanswered questions are connected with the double; yet, they may slowly become transparent here. Not only will this chapter deal with them, but solutions will be approached in the following considerations.

In his brochure, "Der Doppelgänger des Menschen," the physician, Werner Christian Simonis, describes how an attentive observer can often experience the departure of the double shortly before death:

> Who among us has not had the experience that, due to a serious illness, a man fights for his life for a long time and is tortured and shaken by the worst symptoms. All at once, a remarkable calm sets in. Everybody has hope again. The patient himself is as if transformed, more composed and agreeable. Those around him hope that recovery has begun. Three days later the patient dies. What happened here can in most instances be interpreted as the cessation of the double's activity.[79]

The doubles are characterized by Rudolf Steiner as follows:

> These beings spend their lives making use of human beings in order to be present in the domain where they wish to be present. They possess an extraordinarily high intelligence and a very remarkable will, but no feeling heart, no "Gemüt" at all, not what is called human heart and soul. And we do go through life with our soul and such a double. . . .[80]

When we think this over and study contemporary civilization in the light of these insights, we realize to what extent these Doppelgänger-beings have shaped our civilization in their image. People of our time have developed high intelligence and have the strong will to shape earthly life according to their ideas. Since the 15th, 16th, and particularly since the middle of the 19th century, our culture has been formed based on these two faculties. To the degree that thinking and will grew, the forces of the human middle, the rhythmic system, withered. Not only the warm heart forces in the human being, but likewise the creative soul forces, linked as they are with the human rhy mic system, were stunted. Along with them, artistic and moral-religious forces as well as socially unifying forces wasted away. Mankind's heart died. Our age fully reveals the nature of the double. To a large extent, the double has suceeded in extinguishing the human middle-system, and with it people's artistic nature. And so, through the double, Ahriman became lord of contemporary civilization.

It is extremely important to recognize this. The double is of Ahrimanic nature. Through the intellect and earth-directed will, it tries to unite the human being with the lower earth forces. In his lectures, "The New Spirituality and the Christ Experience," Rudolf Steiner speaks of three different types of beings who under all circumstances wish to prevent the break-through to a new spirituality in the Western part of the world. The first type is described as follows: "The first type are spirits who have a special attraction to what, in a sense, are the elemental forces of the earth. . . ."[81] The elemental forces issue from beings who owe their forces to the earth. They are soul-beings but possess no ego. The double also is of this kind. It wishes to push human beings down to the level of intelligent soul-beings, who are not led by their own ego but by a spiritual being active from outside, or the latter's representative on earth. This has significant social consequences, especially in the West.

As was said, the double brings it about that human beings primarily open up to the earth forces. This occurs in unconscious depths of soul. More tightly than they should, human beings are thus chained to the lower forces of the earth, the forces of the ground. They then tend to see the world from the viewpoint of the physical earth, meaning, they see it materialistically; they live more strongly in the blood and race and overestimate the influence of external conditions on the human being. In the soul's depth, the double acquires an ever greater power over the human unconscious will-nature, his passions, instincts, and destructive tendencies. The human being can thus reveal two totally different sides of his being: he can express his normal nature, yet likewise a completely different one that is also present in him. The double can be active in a person based on sources that he/she is unaware of, yet based on activity which the double is very conscious of. In his novel, *The Strange Case of Dr. Jekyll and Mr. Hyde*, R. L. Stevenson described this.

We can use a recent example here, which at the same time can demonstrate the enormous social effect of the double's nature. During World War II, I became acquainted with a leading Nazi of a small town. National Socialism with its theories of blood, race, and soil, its emphasis on the concept of heredity, the demand for blind obedience to the Führer, and Hitler's idea that only the community, the group, is important, not the single individual, was a pure manifestation of the double's nature. During the period when Anthroposophy and its daughter-movements were forbidden, I worked in my brother's firm. He often had to deal with this prominent Nazi. We were invited one day to his house. In the course of the conversation, he asked me whether I had Communist leanings. I replied, "No, certainly not," and explained to him my spiritual views of the world and humanity as well as my religious conviction. This led him to tell me that he had once studied theology, but had later given it up. Thus we discovered a common interest and talked to each other in a free, open manner about spiritual questions. Gradually, it became obvious that this private conversation was connected after all with an official order. He was supposed to determine whether I was identical with a Communist of the same name. He became convinced that I was somebody else. Afterwards, he invited us to his private quarters and we came to know him within the family circle. There, he was a completely relaxed, unassuming, and loving father and husband. It was hard to believe that, in his official capacity, this man was a totally different person. Imbued with the spirit of Hitler, he was cold, haughty, and without any human compassion for dissidents. In a towering rage, he could hit a prisoner on the head with his cane. It never became more obvious to me that, in addition to the actual person, another being can inhabit that person and completely dominate him or her.

The double works in the most diverse ways in and through the human being. Its working could be clearly observed in the case of Charles Manson, who had the actress Sharon Tate and her friends murdered in California. I experienced this crime as a sign that the double has succeeded in a more powerful breakthrough in the West. During his earlier years, Charles Manson made use of his time in prison by eagerly studying the Bible, especially John's Revelation. In it, he was drawn—characteristically—to the figure of Apollyon, the angel of the abyss, even depicting himself once as Apollyon.

In the Apocalypse, Apollyon is the group spirit, the angelic leader of the locusts. It goes without saying that the latter are not locusts like those one comes across in nature, for it says of them that they are not to harm grass, nor trees, nor anything green, only to do harm to human beings. What kind of locusts do that? They are armed as if for war, but have human countenances. They only appear as a group, as masses, not as single individual beings, not as ego-bearers. They are humans that look like humans, yet are only instinctively acting group-soul-beings who in reality are directed by a group-spirit. A letter that Manson addressed to the court clearly brings to expression that he felt driven by something that worked in him: "I have my own law, it works in me." This letter moreover shows how strongly he was imbued with thoughts from the Apocalypse: "I have spoken with the sign that I wish to bear on my forehead." One can confuse the double in oneself with God: "The god is movement, and I am a witness."[82] The Apocalypse refers not only to the sign of God on the forehead but likewise to the sign of the beast. If we do not find a spiritual force today that is capable of standing up to the double, then a part of humanity will fall prey to the downward-drawing forces and turn into beings with the sign of the beast, into locusts.

Charles Manson, who was intelligent and had a strong, although instinctive will, possessed a strange power over those who were connected with him, young people of male and even more of female gender. They blindly obeyed him. Frequently, they were young people from good families. Some had attended university. They formed a large family with Charles Manson as head. Some girls later described how they initially experienced Manson as the embodiment of goodness, one who had to fulfill God's will on earth, but then increasingly as the angel of death who was in the service of evil. This, however, did not frighten them away. Manson was driven by an inner power, when the horrible crime was perpetrated. He took a few of his "family members" with him, mostly girls. They went on their way without knowing whom they wanted to murder, simply driven by Charles Manson's unconscious instinct. They entered some houses and left them again until they finally came to Sharon Tate's home. They killed everybody they encountered there. At the location of the crime, they were gripped by a blind will of destruction. Pregnant Sharon Tate was murdered by numerous knife stabs. This action is so incomprehensible that book upon book has been written about it, seeking for a solution of the riddle. But from the earthly aspect, it cannot be solved.

When we live completely in the physical-sensory world with our conceptions and feelings, something the double aims for, this has certain consequences for us. Rudolf Steiner states:

> I pointed out what happens to people who, at present here on the physical plane, absorb only conceptions that derive from the sense world or are acquired by the intellect, an intellect that is tied to the sense world and declines to know anything aside from the sense world. After their death, people like these are bound, as it were, to an environment that is still strongly linked to the earthly, physical region where human beings sojourn between birth and death.

Because of their life within the physical body, such people remain spellbound after death for a long time to the mortal material world, and through them destructive forces are generated within this physical world. One touches upon profound, significant secrets of human life with matters such as these. . . .[83]

In a public lecture in St. Gallen that preceded the lecture to members concerning the double, the following description was given:

One who, due to his purely physical consciousness, condemns himself to remain in the world of matter, turns into a center of destructive forces that intrude into events which occur in human life and the world. As long as we are within the body, we can entertain merely sensory thoughts . . . : the body is a protection. . . . But when we enter the spiritual world with merely physical conceptions, we turn into centers of destruction.[84]

In the course of the last few years, we have experienced a significant increase in destructive forces on earth. We can see in them the effect by human beings who, prepared by the double, became sources of destruction for the physical world after their death, for their influences reach back to the earth. (Just think of the increase of violent crimes in America!)

In order to understand the specific activity of the double in America, we have to remember that the double is not active in the same way all over the world:

These Ahrimanic-Mephistophelian beings, who take hold of humans shortly before they are born, have very specific preferences of their own. There are those who prefer the Eastern hemisphere, Europe, Asia,

Africa; they choose people who will be born there in order to make use of their bodies. Others select bodies that are born in the Western hemisphere, in America.[85]

This depends on the deeper geographic conditions. Rudolf Steiner says of Russia:

In Eastern Europe, relatively little inclination is due purely to what streams out of the earth. The Russian people . . . are intimately linked together because of their land; they take up very special forces from out of the ground, forces that do not originate from the earth.[86]

The double is therefore active in different ways in different parts of the world. In America, the significant point is that the double unites and permeates human beings especially with those forces that stream exclusively from the earth itself.

On the one side, they are forces of mechanization: "America's intention is to mechanize everything. . . ."[87] This is connected with the fact that the metabolic-limb system dominates in Western human beings. In Rudolf Steiner's last letter of his *Letters to the Members,* dealing with "Nature and Sub-Nature," he writes:

Human beings become linked to certain earth forces by directing their organism toward those forces. We learn to stand and walk upright; we learn to place ourselves with arms and hands into the balance of earthly forces. Now *these* forces are not of the kind that send their effects down from the cosmos. They are *purely* earthly ones. . . . We speak of mechanical laws. We believe that we have abstracted them from the contexts of nature. But this is not the case.

All purely mechanical laws that we perceive mentally have been experienced inwardly through our orientation within the physical world (through standing, walking, and so on). This classifies mechanical matters as purely earthly ones.

When these earthly forces are kept in check by cosmic forces, they serve us. But if we fall under their spell, we lose our balance and they fetter us to the earth's sub-nature, ". . . and that is not *nature*, it is *sub-nature*, a world which in the downward direction becomes emancipated from nature."[88]

The relationship of Western humanity to electricity and earth-magnetism is a different one. One of the most influential founding fathers of the United States of America, Benjamin Franklin, studied the phenomena of electricity for years, made a number of discoveries, and received recognition from several universities. He is considered to be the founder of the science of electricity. We need only think of the significant role that electricity plays today in technology. There is yet another important aspect of electricity that Rudolf Steiner refers to:

> In the 19th century, natural science discovered that the nervous system is permeated by electrical forces. This was correct; natural science was right. But if science believes . . . that the nervous energy, which we possess and which is the basis of our conceptual life, has anything to do at all with electrical currents that pass through the nerves, it is indeed mistaken. For the electrical currents are the forces that are placed into our being by the being that I have just described; it is not at all part of our being. . . .[89]

It is the double that dwells in the currents of electricity which science was able to verify in the human nervous system.

Through them, this double stands in a relationship to all the electromagnetic earth forces. We are only familiar with the outer effects of electricity; its inner nature remains hidden to us. Even as all the earth's forces have a soul-spiritual side, so too the electromagnetic forces. Electricity is imbued with a shadowy replica of soul elements. Our abstract thinking has likewise become shadowy as compared to living thinking. Despite its shadowy nature, those forces that compress the human soul and cut people off from the spirit penetrate through it. They are the antisocial forces that divide human beings.

There is an inner connection between the compressing force of intellectual thinking and electricity. The nerve-sense organization is the bearer of thinking; in this organization, science has ascertained electrical currents. Electricity is a force of nature, but it possesses yet another aspect aside from the shadow of soul-elements, and this is evil: "Moral impulses, natural impulses flow within electricity—but they are the immoral instincts of evil. . . ."[90]

In Goethe's age, no wires existed that passed through the landscape in order to conduct electrical power to towns and factories. There were no electrical appliances that are changing our lives even in the kitchen. There were no radios, nor television that constantly affect us, no electric light that changes night into day for us. In those days, human beings still had a soul-relationship to the spirit of nature and to spiritual things in general, even though not in a new way. Human beings today are radically cut off from the spirit and invaded through and through by materialism.

If people are exposed too strongly to the electromagnetic forces, they lose their connection with the true spiritual world. They lose the possibility of recognizing their true spiritual being in themselves and become completely dependent on the earth. In his brochure, *Geheimnisvolle Erde*, Berthold Wulf speaks of this:

> Every organ that is conversely organized under the influence of the soul element, is a bearer of electrical energy, the shadow of the soul's elements. We said that this applies particularly to the substance of the nerves. Now, one element, which has a connection to electricity, is especially important for the nerves' substance, namely phosphorus. Both electricity and phosphorus have the tendency to compress; on the other hand, both emit light. The nerves' substance consists of phosphoric protein. The very substance of the nerves is predisposed to transmit light as well as light's residue, its ash, namely, electricity.[91]

Thus, a force that compresses man and hardens his soul proceeds from all electromagnetic elements.

Rudolf Steiner stresses that what applies to America does not equally apply to Europe or Russia:

> The region, where above all those magnetic forces rise up that bring human beings into a relationship to this double, was known to be in America. For the most evident relationships to the double originate from that region on earth that is covered by the American continent. . . . The region where the forces stream upward that have the most influence on the double; where, in the double, they enter into the closest relationship with what streams out, hence, where in turn they are imparted again to the earth; this is the region where most of the mountain ranges do not run horizontally from west to east but predominantly from north to south. For this, too, is connected with these forces. . . .[92]

Which mountain ranges in America run chiefly from north to south? They are the Rocky Mountains that divide eastern America from the west; likewise, the mountain ranges of the Sierra Nevada and the Pacific coastal mountains that run through California. All these mountain ranges run in the direction of Mexico. The continuation of the Rockies runs through Mexico and South America. In his book on America, von Cles describes the scenery and in so doing refers to the extraordinarily strong electricity in some regions:

> In the mountainous areas, the electricity in the air is so powerful that especially installed signs warn of touching metal objects. Even during a casual hand-shake, one can receive a painful electric shock that makes one jerk back.[93]

I believe that von Cles describes an experience he had, but one that is rarely encountered with such force. It does not mean that such electricity is evident only in the mountainous areas, but likewise in other areas where mountain ranges take such a direction. In the deserts of America, strong electrical effects can be detected as well.

Furthermore, the double is connected with the origin of illnesses that arise out of man's inner being:

> This double is no more and no less than the cause of all physical illnesses that arise spontaneously out of the inner organism. To know this double fully is to practice organic medicine.[94]

Rudolf Steiner calls special attention to the fact that a physician, who can take seriously what he says about the double, has to expect that differing forces arise from various geographic locations on earth, that they can influence human beings and make them ill.

Furthermore, one of the most important tasks of the future will be, once more to cultivate and advance geographic medicine which had ceased to exist . . . .[95]

Karl Buchleitner deals with this subject in an article, "Spirituelle Medizin und der Doppelgänger." Buchleitner emphasizes the social effects of the double:

These doubles moreover work in an inspirational way into our social structures. They try to paralyze the soul's own spiritual force, to replace it with purely intellectual thinking. Wherever experiments are conducted with human beings, it occurs under the influence of the double. It is all-important for the social life, as well as for medicine, to see through the intentions of these beings.[96]

In the brochure mentioned earlier, *Der Doppelgänger des Menschen*, Simonis demonstrates the importance of Rudolf Steiner's lecture concerning the secret of the double for a medicine of the future. After he has summed up six of the most important "characteristics of the Ahrimanic double living in the human being," he goes on:

Up to now, the indications by the spiritual researcher have enabled us to follow the ways in which the double's nature is connected with a person from the very beginning of life. This results in a certain "physiology" of this being and on occasion a "pathology" for human beings. Furthermore, we must be mindful that these effects of knowing or being ignorant of these relationships have decisive importance for every human being.[97]

If one wishes to become informed about the medical aspects dealing with the double, one should read what the two physicians, Buchleitner and Simonis, have written about it in an introductory way. Particularly in America, knowledge of the double is especially important on account of the social consequence. These forces naturally affect *every* human being, whether he or she knows it or not, but they work more strongly in those who have no awareness of this. In the future, it will become necessary to distinguish between what comes from people themselves and what comes from the double in them, otherwise one will be unable to heal them. Many severe mental problems, depressions and the like, destructive qualities in the soul, inclinations that manifest in the soul of leading a purely materialistic life, an aversion or hatred against anything spiritual—all this has to do with the double in us, hence with the power that tries to link us only to the lower forces of the earth. People will seek for the causes of their depression elsewhere, and it will be impossible to heal them. Not only physicians, but anybody who has to deal with people in a religious, social, educational, or criminal regard should have accurate knowledge of the double's activity. Why did young Americans by the thousands and tens-of-thousands crowd into movie theaters to see "The Exorcist," a film made after the book by William Peter Blatty?[98] The title page of the book proclaimed: "The Bestselling Novel of Demonic Possession." Young people in their subconscious sensed the presence of a being that did not belong to them, namely, their own double. They sought clarification for what was going on within themselves. Instead, they watched the expulsion of a demon. But the double does not allow itself to be driven out.

Comprehension of the double's nature and activity must be recognized as a significant task. We have to realize that the forces, which have to do with the geographic conditions in the East, the Middle, and the West, can overpower us if we are not watchful. We must know that the forces which arise from the ground in America have nothing, nothing whatsoever to do with the West's inner predisposition. These are two quite unrelated matters.

Are there healing powers for us, powers that can create a balance with the forces that powerfully draw us downward toward the earth's interior? The healing impulses are contained in what ensouled Emerson and his friends. To unite oneself with the spirit of humanity—this is what America with its inhabitants from all over the world needs, but today in an advanced, conscious manner. One of the truly most fundamental insights attained through Anthroposophy is that, since the Event on Golgotha, Christ has become the Spirit of Humanity. Christ *is* the Spirit of Humanity. If this could be experienced by more and more people, not only through their thinking but their heart and will, ever new healing forces could stream from out of this fact. More than anything else, we must become aware today of the presence of the Christ and His healing activity.

HEALING FORCES OF HYGIENIC OCCULTISM

The development of spiritual healing forces is decisive for the rehabilitation of our culture. The faculty of hygienic occultism can unfold from the predispositions of Central European humanity. This will be of importance for the whole world. Consciousness is only possible through decline and destruction in the physical organization. Illness between birth and death is likewise connected with this. The constructive, health-promoting forces, those that cause growth and life, the healing forces, they all are, as we saw, related to the will forces. Rudolf Steiner states: "The healing force inherent in the human organism turns to occult esoteric insights, if transformed into cognition."[99]

The force in question is one that up until now has not been transformed in humanity. We first had to develop our present-day consciousness and illuminate it with spiritual light in order to be able to utilize these healing forces through an elevation of consciousness. We could also say that, through the transformation of the forces of perception and knowledge, through earnest anthroposophical study, forces unfold: "This hygienic occult faculty is well on its way and, relatively speaking, will not keep us waiting too long."[100]

When thinking—enlivened and strengthened by the will, and will illuminated by spiritual thinking—meet in the human heart, then the spiritualized heart blossoms forth and sends healing ether-streams through human words and deeds. In order to develop this healing power of consciousness, no feelings of antipathy, not to mention feelings of hatred, may arise in a person against other human beings or nations. Such emotions would destroy his or her occult healing force. As cognizant ones, free of antipathy or sympathy, we must confront others with spiritual love. Cognitive love, above all, allows the healing occult force in us to grow. Hygienic occultism will penetrate spiritually oriented medicine; it will grow and mature through the dedicated work with children in need of special curative care. Hygienic occultism will stream through the creative word and formative work of artistically active people and those who are involved in social and educational domains, emitting harmonizing, constructive, healing spiritual force. Today, we are only at the beginning of this development, but at last it will become more strongly effective. Eurythmy will play an important role in America, because Americans are people whose limb-organism is particularly pronounced. They love movement and activities of the limbs, of which sports are ample proof. Notably in young Americans lives a longing and strong inclination not only to be involved in sports and physical activity, but rhythmically and artistically, in consciously formed movements. Some seek their life's calling in the study of eurythmy and later become eurythmy teachers and performing artists. Not only will curative eurythmy produce healing forces; healing powers will also stream through artistic eurythmy. Instruction and performances will have curative, healing effects on people. Strong healing power will one day stream out from new, timely religious rites, when the acting priests pursue their inner meditative path in an increasingly devoted manner and imbue themselves more and more powerfully with Anthroposophy.

It is important to realize that people of the East, the West, and the Middle are not only capable of allowing their own predispositions to mature but to acquire those of the others. But the latter must be developed consciously. They do not develop by themselves, not out of people's own potential faculty. This is particularly significant for the West, where the forces of the Ahrimanic double strengthen intellectual thinking and the earth-oriented will, but allow the heart forces to weaken. No predisposition exists in the West for developing the healing power of the spiritualized heart. Here, that power must be consciously cultivated. This becomes possible, if more and more facilities are established in the West where Anthroposophy is cultivated, as is even now the case in a number of locations. This will allow the forces of healing occultism to mature. Anthroposophy is not only a body of teachings. It is a curative remedy for the needs and dangers in the West.

If the Mystery of Golgotha had not taken place, says Rudolf Steiner, the doubles of the human beings would long since have become the lords of the earth. This throws light on the kind of help the West requires; for the human heart can be spiritualized by the power of the Mystery of Golgotha. It can develop healing forces that limit and overcome the ill-boding effect of the double. The Christ-powers were infused into the whole earth. They are present as a predisposition in the West as well. We are now approaching the Second Coming of the Christ. Can this event offer the West decisive help?

The Second Golgotha Event
in the Nineteenth Century

In the supersensible world, invisible to human senses and directly adjacent to the earthly realm, an event of the greatest importance took place in recent times. A sort of repetition of the Golgotha Event occurred there, not as was the case then in the physical form of a man, but in the etheric spirit-body of an angelic being. Since His Resurrection through the Event of Golgotha, Christ is active in the form of this angelic being in the etheric spirit-domain of the earth. In his Damascus experience, Paul was the first human being who was able to perceive Him in this angelic form.

During the 19th century, in this angelic being, Christ suffered an extinction of His consciousness. There is no death in the spiritual world like there is on earth, but a deathlike experience, namely, the extinction of a spirit-being's consciousness. Christ experienced this in the ether-world as a second Golgotha Event. Call to mind that an angelic being has a consciousness quite different from that of a human being. It is a far more all-encompassing consciousness, because it is not limited by a physical body. It possesses the faculty of consciousness and range of an etheric body. Angelic consciousness encompasses the earth's ether body. On that account, it accompanies all etheric spirit-events of the earth and humanity as if they were its own. Christ is likewise united with the earth and humankind through this etheric angel-consciousness. Because of this, He can spiritually accomplish what He wishes to do with the earth and especially humanity. He slowly tries to lead both by means of a new spirit-revelation toward a more spiritualized state. This could only happen through a new sacrifice. Rudolf Steiner explains in the lecture "Christ at the Time of the Mystery of Golgotha and Christ in the 20th Century," in London, that people who died in the 19th century, who imbued themselves during life on earth only with materialistic thoughts and sentiments, bore the latter up into the ether world. They darkened this world. This led to an extinction of the angelic being's consciousness:

> Even though Christ came into the ancient Hebrew race and there was led to His death, the angelic being, that since then has been the outer form of the Christ, suffered an extinction of consciousness in the course of the 19th century as a result of the contradictory materialistic forces that had risen into the spiritual worlds. . . .[101]

Here, we should associate this with the doubles of the human beings, who fetter them to the earth and in so doing make them susceptible to materialism. This always has a cosmic effect as well.

During the mighty turning-point that took place almost 2,000 years ago in humanity, when the blood of Christ Jesus flowed from the cross and united with the earth; when, turning into dust, the body of Christ Jesus was given over to the earth's elements, Christ, the lofty Sun Spirit, united Himself with earth evolution. Through this exalted sacrificial deed, the earth received into her being the seed for becoming a new Sun. As the body of the Christ, she became the source of a new evolution. Since then, Christ is insolubly linked with humanity. He united with humanity's destiny, suffering it as His own, freely willed fate. All ancient karmic effects led humankind downward into the physical world. As the new shaper of human destiny, Christ guides us upward again to a new spirit-experience. With this began the great turning-point in humanity's evolution. At the moment of Christ's death, so the Gospels tell it, the curtain leading to the Holiest of Holy in the Temple, which was accessible only once a year to the high priest, tore open. Along with the tearing of the curtain, the Holiest of Holy in the Temple, in which ancient initiations were carried out, became accessible to all. With this began humanity's pathway to Christ, a new path of initiation that leads through death to spiritual resurrection.

Since Golgotha, insolubly linked with humanity in their very depths of soul, Christ once more treads the path of initiation through death to resurrection, but now *in* humanity. First He leads humanity into the valley of death, for only there can human beings find freedom and their own ego, which is supposed to rise again from death. Once more, He passes through all the stages of the Passion in and with humanity:

The *Washing of the Feet* during the first three to four centuries of Christian development.

The *Scourging* by the Roman soldiers when, in the fourth century, Christianity became a state religion in the Roman Empire, whose spirit began to pervade Christianity.

The *Crowning with the Crown of Thorns*, the pressing of the painful thorns into Christ's head, when Arabism and religious Islam invaded the Occident in order, prematurely, to present to it the intellect, something that culminated in the "abolishing" of the spirit of the human being at the Council of Constantinople.

The *Carrying of the Cross up to the Place of the Skull*, when intellectual head-thinking came about, which produced materialism.

The *Death on Golgotha*, when materialism in the 19th century became predominant in human souls, who in turn bore

117

this materialism up into the spiritual world, there to bring about the second Golgotha Event, the extinction of the Christ-consciousness in the etheric world.

And yet, in all these occidental death-experiences, the fruit of the Christ-deed at the beginning of the Christian era ripened: our own thinking that led to present-day consciousness of self, a consciousness that increasingly becomes capable of recognizing—and thus bringing to birth—the human Spirit-I.

Here, we arrive at the stage of *Resurrection* that now occurs within humanity.

It is deeply moving to read the words of Rudolf Steiner:

> And the beginning of unconsciousness in the spiritual worlds, in the manner just described, will become the resurrection of the Christ-consciousness in the human souls on earth between birth and death in the 20th century.[102]

Let these significant words resound and affect our hearts a little longer: The angelic consciousness in the etheric world is suffused by Christ-consciousness. Due to the materialistic darkening on earth, the Christ-consciousness is extinguished in the angelic being! This is an invisible, yet mighty happening behind the course of outer events, an event that determines our age, even though human beings are completely unaware of it. Following the extinction of the Christ-consciousness in the spiritual world, there begins, as it were, the resounding of the last and most powerful trumpet from the Apocalypse. It proclaims the awakening of the Christ-consciousness in the human being (not of the Christ-experience which has always been present). Christ transforms the dying angel-consciousness in the etheric world and thus begins the resurrection of Christ-consciousness in human beings. This is the truly great, indeed the mighty aspect of our age: human beings become capable of thinking angelic thoughts, spirit-thoughts, on earth. Christ-thoughts become human thoughts. And these thoughts bear not only the light of knowledge, they harbor the world-healing forces of the Christ-being in themselves. With the resurrection of the Christ-consciousness, beginning in the 20th century, healing forces are streaming into the word, through the word, through all that the Christ-imbued human being does. Hygienic occultism can only come to life if Christ resurrects in the human being. And this is what the West needs most urgently.

A more light-filled age is beginning:

> Twice already, Christ has been crucified; the first time physically in the earthly world at the beginning of the Christian era; a second time spiritually in the 19th century in the way it was described. One could say, humanity experienced the resurrection of His body during the first time. It will experience the resurrection of His consciousness beginning in the 20th century.[103]

This way, a tremendous step forward is taken in humanity's evolution in the 20th century. We must be clear about the difference between the resurrection in the body and that in the consciousness of the human being. Then we know without a doubt that Anthroposophy is a kindling of the new Christ-consciousness in humankind. Pursuing these thoughts further, something of great importance is connected with it. We can ask: Does the angelic consciousness remain extinguished in the etheric world? How are we then to understand the etheric Coming of the Christ? When the thoughts that are enkindled in the human being by the descending Christ-consciousness are reflected back to the etheric world or are borne up into these realms by the dead who imbued themselves during life with the spirit, then spiritual light once more spreads out there. And since angelic consciousness envelops this etheric world, it awakens in the light of these human thoughts to a new, elevated etheric consciousness. By passing through human beings, these thoughts become something other than what they were before.

To begin with, we receive spirit-insight into our abstract, lifeless thinking. But because of this, we can receive them in freedom; they do not force us in any way. We must enliven them from out of ourselves if they are to become effective. And this we can do only by activating our thinking through the ego. The enlivening of spiritual thoughts out of the ego transforms them into new, stronger, and better formed thoughts. Through these reflected or upward-carried thoughts, the angelic consciousness awakens on a higher level in the etheric world. Only then does this thinking become the instrument, the being through which the etherically returning Christ can be effective for the future of humankind. Thus, the resurrection of Christ-consciousness in the human being leads to a resurrection in the etheric world. Two things belong together: the resurrection of Christ-consciousness in humanity and the etheric Coming of the Christ. It is an all-surpassing and penetrating event, the most important one after the Mystery of Golgotha: "This is the greatest secret of our age: the secret of Christ's return. . . ."[104]

The spirit-cognizing human being is connected to this event, namely, through the initiate who was in a position to receive into himself the cosmic angel-wisdom, the initiation-knowledge. Rudolf Steiner was the first human being on earth in whom the new Christ-consciousness lit up, the first who could transform it and give it back—already during his life on earth and after his death: "We may therefore consider what we have received as spiritual science as *living Christ-revelation*."[105]

THE ETHERIC COMING OF CHRIST

Concerning the dead who extinguish the Christ-consciousness of the angelic being in the etheric world, Rudolf Steiner says that they "are those who since the 16th century have passed through the portal of death," and that these dead "position themselves against the Christ."[106] Since the 16th century, but especially since the middle of the 19th century, Ahriman prepares his undertaking at the beginning of the third millennium by stronger means. The Ahrimanic beings had been unsuccessful in ultimately extinguishing the Christ-consciousness in the angelic being through the dead, for it did light up once again in the world of humanity. Now the Ahrimanic beings try all they can to stifle it in human souls by the turn of the century, which coincides with the turn of the millennium. They attempt this by means of the significant preparations intended to facilitate Ahriman's personal intervention. Human beings are supposed to be primed in such a way that they become incapable of receiving and absorbing spiritual ideas or to lift themselves up to the perception of Christ's etheric appearance. Ahriman fears nothing so much as an actual link between the human being and the Christ, for such a link could foil many of his intentions.

It is therefore a necessity for us to become fully aware of the significance of the etheric Coming of Christ in our age. This awareness could be the greatest help for a realization of this important event. Rudolf Steiner stated: "At the beginning, only a few, then an ever growing number of people will be able, during the 20th century, to behold the appearance of the Etheric Christ, meaning, to behold Him in the form of an angel."[107] As an important beginning of this new beholding of the Christ in the ether-world, Rudolf Steiner indicated the years 1930, 1933, 1935, 1937 to 1940, more rarely to 1945. "Quite special faculties will then become evident as natural predispositions in human beings."[108] It is remarkable that he refers to these "special faculties" as natural predispositions. This means that special faculties will appear among human beings of the present, which he terms "new" faculties:

> The first intimations of these new soul-faculties will become discernible in a number of souls within a relatively short time. And they will become more evident in the middle of the thirties, approximately between 1930 and 1940.[109]

Still, as early as 1924, he warned of the emergence of the apocalyptic beast in the year 1933. He foresaw what would happen in the outer dimension of history. Through the seizure of power in 1933 in Germany, National Socialism assumed the rule. It plunged the whole world into the worst war that ever befell humanity. In the suppression and persecution of those who dissented, in the ups and downs of wartime chaos, the lamentations and jubilations of alternating defeats and victories, the killing of millions of Jews, and the breakdown and destruction of whole cities through bombing raids by enemy aircraft, the unfolding of the new predisposition and faculties was prevented.

> Two things could happen. One is that, while human beings have the predisposition for this clairvoyance, materialism will be victorious during the next few decades and humankind will sink into the materialistic morass. The other scenario could be that spiritual science will not be struck down.[110]

The result of that would be that the new predispositions and faculties would be recognized and cultivated. In the years mentioned, from 1933 to 1940 or 1945, Anthroposophy was forbidden in Central Europe. Only a handful of people on earth could have met the etherically appearing Christ with any comprehension.

We know that the dead can likewise experience the appearance of the Christ in angelic form:

> . . . Those, however, who then will no longer be alive, but have prepared themselves through spiritual scientific discipline, will nonetheless behold Him in His etheric garment between their death and a new birth.[111]

Since 1911 when this lecture was given, many people, often significant personalities who had prepared themselves through spiritual science, have gone through death. Many individuals may in this way have had a vision of the Etheric Christ in angelic form after their death. Moreover, through Rudolf Steiner, who united himself with the Anthroposophical Society during the Christmas Conference, this mighty event *did not* bypass the Anthroposophical Society. On the contrary, it became the most important organ for a comprehension of the Christ's reappearing on earth. It carries the possibility of making this event fruitful for humanity.

Here, we have to call to mind that Rudolf Steiner not only spoke of new faculties and predispositions that mature in a natural manner in every person. He also spoke of a conscious development of new clairvoyant faculties through esoteric discipline: ". . . we must distinguish between purposely induced clairvoyance and a natural form of clairvoyance that will come about. . . ."[112] The clairvoyance that originates through anthroposophical schooling has an inner connection to the fact that new clairvoyant faculties are beginning to develop in the whole of humanity. "Through what we term esoteric schooling, these clairvoyant faculties will be acquired much more readily."[113] The new predispositions and faculties that lead to the vision of the etherically appearing Christ, can, through inner anthroposophical schooling, lead even to a conscious vision of Christ in His etheric form. A time will come when that will happen, and *with that*, humanity will be given a new opportunity to make up for what it has neglected to do.

One should have a clear idea about the "natural faculties" of a new clairvoyance. For this is not a matter of ancient faculties that people here or there still have; these are new faculties that are arising in the Age of Light. This is likewise implicit in the following words by Rudolf Steiner:

> A number of souls will have a remarkable experience. They will possess ego-consciousness, but in addition it will be for them as if they lived in a world that actually is quite another world from that of their ordinary consciousness: shadowy, like a presentiment, as if one born blind were operated.[114]

New spiritual forces are referred to, forces that unfold in a natural manner. These natural faculties that are trying to emerge are present in *every* human being, but they can be enhanced considerably in a person through conscious schooling. We can acquire a more concrete view of these new natural faculties that develop in human souls as if on their own, meaning, without any special schooling, if we remember that, through the Mystery of Golgotha, a revitalization of the etheric body became possible. The etheric body can thus acquire a force of its own that makes it independent of the physical body.

Through that, it can loosen itself again from the body and strive beyond its limitations.

Up until the end of the Atlantean time, the human etheric body had a loose connection with the physical body. It extended beyond the latter and thus could preserve its ancient clairvoyance. Subsequently, it began to coincide with the physical body in more and more human beings. The etheric head, in particular, became one with the physical head. Rudolf Steiner describes it as follows in the Kassel cycle dealing with the Gospel of John:

> So long as the ether-body was outside the human head, it was in quite a different position than later on. It was connected on all sides with streams, with other spiritual beings, and what flowed in and out there gave the human etheric body the faculty of clairvoyance in Atlantean times.[115]

Beginning with the close of the Atlantean Epoch, physical and etheric bodies came to coincide:

> Whereas the configuration between etheric and physical body has solidified more and more in the course of this epoch up until our own time, becoming inwardly more solid and closely linked, the human being approaches a period in the future when the etheric body will gradually loosen itself again and become independent. The process will be reversed again. Even today, there are those who have much looser etheric bodies than others. This loosening of the etheric body is proper only if the human being has absorbed so much during the various incarnations in the cultural epochs we mentioned that, once his etheric body leaves its confines again, it takes along suitable fruits from the physical sense realm, fruits fitting

to be incorporated into the increasingly independent etheric body.[116]

It is important to see that this loosening and vitalization of the etheric body is connected with Christ:

> At the moment Christ appeared, the etheric body began to emerge once more, and today it is even less connected to the physical body than it was at the time of Christ's presence [on earth]. Through this process, the physical body has become even coarser. Now, the human being is approaching a future when the etheric body will lift itself out more and more. Gradually, there will come the time when the etheric body will extend out as far as it did in Atlantean times.[117]

At that moment, new clairvoyant sight will be possible among human beings. This loosening of the etheric body will occur for all human beings. It will be a proper loosening for all those who in their previous earthly incarnations have acquired "proper fruits from the . . . earthly world," namely for those, in whom the effects of the Christ-experience on earth will have born "proper fruits." We can picture it as follows: In those who pursue an esoteric path—who do not simply take the Christ-consciousness, which has died down in the etheric world, into their souls but into their consciousness—the etheric part of the human head can loosen in a more correct way from the physical body. In so doing, it can then ascend to a consciously beheld perception of the etherically appearing Christ. In those who initially can accept the new Christ-forces only into their soul, these forces can strengthen the awakening of the new, natural clairvoyant abilities. Souls like these will likewise have an opportunity to meet the Christ and later to find the way to a spiritual, conscious encounter with Him.

In Rudolf Steiner's Mystery Dramas, Theodora, in whom these Christ-forces were powerful, could in this way behold the Christ even before she was on a spiritually conscious path. But she was then led directly to the place where she had the opportunity to accept Christ into her consciousness. What was effective in her prior to that moment, was already the power of Christ.

THE SECOND COMING OF
CHRIST AND OPPOSING ACTIVITIES

A new and greater possibility of beholding the etheric Christ will come to pass with the turn of the century. Even though Rudolf Steiner did not specifically say so in his lectures, it is a necessary, indeed foregone, conclusion from all that he outlined concerning the coming events. For example, the Platonists will descend to earth once again with their great spiritual forces that they were able to develop for centuries in the spiritual world. Others will return to earth who, in the course of the 20th century, were incarnated here. Through accepting and studying spiritual science in that earthly incarnation, they could evolve further in their life after death in order to appear on earth again, with new faculties—for instance, with the ability of recalling their last incarnation. Many of them will have had the vision of the etheric Christ in their life after death.

In several lectures dealing with the etheric appearance of the Christ, Rudolf Steiner pointed out that the pre-Christian times will be repeated following the Golgotha Event, but on a higher level. In the first millennium of our Christian era, the Solomonic epoch was repeated, in the second, that of the age of Moses. Beginning with the third millennium, the repetition of the age of Abraham will commence. He said concerning this: "We are approaching this Abraham-epoch and it must and will bring us mighty events."[118] Abraham was the first human being in whom the forces that were the basis of ancient clairvoyance, were utilized for the inner transformation of his physical-corporeal organization. This produced the physical

instrument of thinking. Through the enhancement of the physical brain, ancient clairvoyance was transformed into conscious forces of thinking. Today, we must move in the opposite direction. The developed thought-forces must become free of the brain so that new clairvoyance can evolve. In connection with the beginning of the third millennium it says: "We are going in a direction that will allow human beings once again to enter into conditions of natural clairvoyance."[119]

This second exalted possibility of beholding Christ in the etheric body should be thoroughly prepared in order to make, what was prevented to a large extent between 1933 and 1945, fruitful for earthly humanity after all. And this should be done despite the fact that we know only too clearly that the Ahrimanic beings will go to even greater lengths this time in order to prevent a breakthrough for beholding the etheric Christ. This process of making matters fruitful for humanity can be enhanced by perceptive inward participation in what constitutes the main event in our age. The following can then ensue for humanity: ". . . beginning in the 20th century, the life of Christ can increasingly be felt as a direct personal experience in human souls."[120] This feeling will appear particularly strongly when we recognize Christ as the lofty Spirit-being who, in our age, wishes to resurrect in human *consciousness*.

Spiritually experiencing the Christ through spirit-awareness, even if it does not lead to actual vision, is already an inner recognition of the etheric Christ. It produces the mood of expectation necessary for Christ's appearance and intervention in the events that we approach.

It was possible in America quite a number of years ago to write a thesis dealing with the Second Coming of Christ. A member of the Anthroposophical Society, who meanwhile has become a Waldorf School teacher, earned her Master's Degree

at California State University Sacramento with a paper on "A Comparison of Some Philosophical Views of W. B. Yeats and Rudolf Steiner with Emphasis on the Second Coming."[121]

She describes similarities of destiny that are evident in both individuals, even though one (Yeats) was born in Ireland and the other (Steiner) in Austria-Hungary. Both had a spiritual world view. Both had associations with the Theosophical Society; they were personally acquainted with A. Besant and other leading members of that society; both were actively involved in this society and both had their own, albeit quite differing, view concerning the Second Coming of Christ in this century. The writer of this paper describes the frequently dreamlike, visionary views of Yeats and the clear, conscious spiritual-scientific thoughts of Rudolf Steiner. She describes how the latter arrived at his views based on his own spiritual perceptions and through a specifically occidental path of knowledge and initiation, and how he represented his views even within the Theosophical Society with its eastern orientation. She describes why Yeats had to leave the society and subsequently concerned himself more with Rosicrucian ideas, and how Rudolf Steiner had to leave because he could not approve of the view that Christ would reappear in the present age in a Hindu youngster. Rudolf Steiner never spoke of a physical-corporeal Second Coming of Christ, only of an etheric-spiritual one. After withdrawing from the Theosophical Society, he founded the Anthroposophical Society. When Yeats was young, he assumed that a spiritual age would begin at the end of the 20th century. He could not maintain this view in old age (he died in 1939). Then, he spoke of a return of the evil world power, the Anti-Christ. In his poem, "Second Coming," he wrote that when he thought of the Second Coming, an image from the Akashic Record (the Cosmic Memory) would upset him, namely, the demonic beast. Twenty centuries after

133

Christ, this beast would be born in our age, namely at the end of this century. He saw the symptoms of the beast's approach in the increase of immorality, a materialistic, spirit-denying world view, the rise of criminality, and so on.

The author of the above thesis gave a detailed outline in her paper on the views derived from modern spiritual science or Anthroposophy, concerning the appearance of the etheric Christ. She moreover depicted, in contrast to Yeats' views, what Rudolf Steiner said about Ahriman's incarnation in the West. She illustrated this by means of statements by Rudolf Steiner. Her thesis was accepted and she received her Master's Degree. In California of all places, surprising openness for spiritual views prevails. Perhaps this is because the East with its great variety of spiritual convictions is well represented here. Of course, this has its negative aspects as well. People already know everything, an attitude that easily prevents them from going more thoroughly into genuine spiritual matters. But when true spirit-insight is missing, the danger grows that, in the place of the reappearing Christ, another being is substituted. Clairvoyant forces are growing in a natural way in human beings. They can lead to the Christ but also can be misused by Ahriman. The forces that can keep Ahriman in check were given to us by the spiritual world in the greatest spiritual event since the Mystery of Golgotha, namely, the spirit-activity of the reappearing Christ.

Imagine what this mighty, all-illuminating event of the etheric Second Coming brings about and what can result from it, if it could freely unfold. When the Christ-consciousness became extinguished in the etheric world, it awoke as a new consciousness, as living thinking in the human being. This thinking began to be effective in all areas of science, art, religion, social and educational life. To anybody with slightly deeper insight, this is an actual effect of Christ's reappearance. We are facing the dawn of a new consciousness. If this consciousness could unfold freely and unhampered in humanity, a new spiritual culture would soon blossom forth from it. People would thus recognize their cosmic nature. In it, they would experience the Spirit-I that passes through all the various incarnations. Their responsibility in regard to earth's evolution would become clear to them. On the one side, they would be earthly human beings; on the other, they would increasingly experience their cosmic human nature with its higher forces. Standing thus between two worlds, between the earthly being and the experience of the cosmic being, will not always be easy to bear:

> This will be the solution to the most formidable disharmony ever to arise in earth-existence: the disharmony of people feeling themselves as earthly beings, and their recognition that they are supersensible, cosmic beings. The fulfillment of this inner urge will prepare people to perceive how, out of grey depths of spirit, this Christ-being will reveal Himself to them. He will now speak to them spiritually, as He spoke to human beings in the physical realm at the time of the Mystery of Golgotha. The Christ will not come in this spiritual sense, if we are not prepared. And we can prepare only in the way just described, namely, by sensing the above-mentioned discrepancy, by feeling the incongruity that weighs on us terribly. . . .[122]

We can free ourselves from this pressure, this weight, if we follow Lucifer's paths and reach bliss in our cosmic experience, or follow Ahriman's paths, if we merely experience ourselves in our earthly human nature. But since we are exposed most powerfully at present to the Ahrimanic danger, the earth's force of attraction will become the most threatening to us. Here, the Ahrimanic world-power can gain a foothold in order to make the etheric Second Coming of the Christ ineffective. More clearly than we do, Ahriman sees the possibilities that Christ's appearance can have for humanity. He recognizes with all clarity that this event poses the greatest danger for everything that he plans for humankind.

Ahriman has been working for centuries on preventing the breakthrough toward the spirit by human beings under the leadership of the etheric Christ Whom Michael serves. Ahriman tries to maintain the thinking that cuts human beings off from the spirit. He hardens our thinking, feeling, and willing in order to bolster materialism on earth. More clearly than we can, Ahriman sees America's openness, for example, to Christ's appearance. He will try to direct the forces of expectation to himself and his appearance. At that time, he will even cause human beings to become clairvoyant—based on *his* powers. But then people will not behold the Christ, but Ahriman. Ahriman's preparations for this will be well thought out, thorough, and most effective. We should not shy away from recognizing Rudolf Steiner's disappointment, when he saw the ineffectiveness of the members of the Anthroposophical Society regarding their preparation for Christ's appearance and their opposition to Ahriman's activity from the spiritual and physical side. At the end of the lectures on "The New Spirituality and the Christ Experience in the Twentieth Century," he spoke of the etheric appearance of the Christ:

> It is not easy to see through these matters with firm resolve, for one always realizes how little people are inclined nowadays to count on thorough, powerful insight. The opponents are on the alert. They develop all the intensity required for doing battle. Our effort, what we are capable of, is weak, very weak, and our concept of Anthroposophy is in many respects

sleepy, very sleepy. This is the greatest pain that over-
comes a person today who fully sees through these
matters.[123]

Rudolf Steiner tried to indicate the seriousness of this new
Christ-experience:

> To the same degree that people will be able to
> sense the Christ-impulse in their souls, solutions to
> our social problems will come about. All other social
> solutions will merely lead to destruction and chaos,
> because all the other solutions point to the description
> of the human being as an earthly being. But human-
> ity is rising above this frame of mind—particularly in
> our time—the frame of mind that allows us to view
> ourselves in our present consciousness as merely
> earthly-physical beings. Out of the disposition of the
> human soul and out of suffering, the new Christ-expe-
> rience will be formed. But then, that much more
> attention must be paid to any and all opposition and
> hindrances that try to prevent the approach of this
> new Christ-experience.[124]

INCARNATIONS OF LUCIFER, CHRIST, AND AHRIMAN

Anthroposophy refers to an incarnation of Lucifer. It occurred at the beginning of the third pre-Christian millennium in the East. In an important mystery center in East Asia, a remarkable child grew up. When he had turned forty, a significant change occurred in him. "Around age forty, this man suddenly began to grasp, purely by human reason, what earlier had infused the mysteries only through revelation."[125] He was able to grasp and comprehend spiritual truths with the organ of the intellect for the first time. Throughout his life, this man remained linked to the mysteries. In him, Lucifer was incarnated.

> It is an important, a significant fact that a corporeal incarnation of Lucifer actually took place in the third pre-Christian millennium in eastern Asia. And from this physical incarnation of Lucifer—for this personality was then a teacher—issued what can really be described as the pagan, pre-Christian culture, one that even imbued Gnosticism in the first Christian centuries.[126]

Rudolf Steiner states that it would be quite wrong to disdain this Lucifer-culture

> . . . for the beauty and philosophical insight that Greece brought forth, and what lives in ancient Greek philosophy and still in the tragedies of Aeschylus—all that would not have been possible without this Lucifer-incarnation.[127]

139

We can see from this, how important Lucifer's incarnation was for all humanity, and that such an incarnation took place in order to introduce something decisive to earthly humanity.

Thereafter, at the turning point of time, Christ's incarnation in the flesh came to pass, the incarnation that gave the whole of humanity's evolution a new direction. In the year 30, Christ incarnated in Jesus of Nazareth. Three years later, the most significant event for humanity occurred, namely, the Mystery of Golgotha.

> To these two incarnations, that of Lucifer in antiquity, and that of Christ which in effect represents earth-evolution's deepest meaning, a third incarnation will be added in a not too distant future. And present events move mainly in the direction of preparing this third incarnation.[128]

The event of Lucifer's incarnation completely eluded human awareness. A little was known of it only in Eastern mysteries. To a large degree, the incarnation of Christ likewise bypassed human consciousness. But under no circumstances should this happen in the case of Ahriman's incarnation in the West: "Human beings must consciously await the Ahriman-incarnation and try increasingly to heighten their awareness."[129]

We live in the age of the consciousness soul. Nothing of significance for humanity may occur in our age without our being fully conscious of it. Unconsciousness would affect humanity disastrously. It is absolutely necessary to make the effort of becoming increasingly aware of Ahriman's activities on earth, because Ahriman will dominate the second half of earth-evolution, even as Lucifer dominated the first half. To an ever growing extent, we will be up against the intervention of Ahrimanic beings here on earth. We cannot afford to remain blind in regard to them:

Since the middle of the Atlantean age, a very different opponent from Lucifer has been approaching humankind. He is the adversary who befogs and darkens the human faculties of perception and knowledge to the end that human beings neither make the effort nor develop the desires to discover the secrets behind the sense world. If we imagine that, due to Lucifer's influence, the sense world became like a veil behind which the spiritual world certainly still existed, then, due to the influence of this second being, this physical world turned completely into something like thick bark that closed itself off against the spiritual world. . . .[130]

We have three very special events in humanity's evolution: Lucifer's incarnation in the flesh, the incarnation of Christ in the flesh, and Ahriman's incarnation in the flesh. The first two incarnations produced mighty changes. What changes will occur through the third incarnation, that of Ahriman? No doubt, significant changes will ensue in humanity's evolution through this third incarnation of a spirit-being on earth. But during this last one, the incarnation of Ahriman, we are called upon to join in intervening in the course of evolution.

As was outlined, the Ahrimanic world power's intention is to harden this earthly world progressively until it has become totally rigid.

We need only consider that the desire of the Ahrimanic forces is to bring the earth to the point of complete rigidity. These forces would have won their game as soon as they would be successful in completely rigidifying everything to do with earth, water, and air.[131]

What can complete rigidity of earth, water, and air refer to? In the lecture, "The Moral Element as the Source of World-Creative Powers," Rudolf Steiner describes how living spiritual thinking works on the body's organism, contrasting it with the effect of rigid intellectual thinking. Living thinking works through its moral ideals in a stimulating way on the human warmth-organism; it produces sources of light (light ether) in the human air-organism and sources of tone (chemical ether) in the fluid organism. In the physical organism, it creates seeds of life. By contrast, intellectual, theoretical thinking causes the warmth-organism to turn cold. It makes the light-sources ineffective, deadens the sources of tone, and extinguishes life. And since the physical processes in the human organism of warmth, air, water, and earth influence the warmth, air, water, and earth-substances of the surroundings of human beings, the actively working spirit-element in warmth, air, water, and earth in the whole physical world is deadened and made rigid. Thus, the earth dies, and with it, the true human being. Human beings would then merely see themselves as beings of nature, no longer as spirit beings. First, they would link themselves in thought, then even in their will, with the animal species. The Ahrimanic beings

do not wish to make human beings particularly spiritual. Their goal is to slay the awareness of our spirituality in us. They would like to teach us the view that the human being is actually just a fully evolved animal. Ahriman is in truth the mighty teacher of materialistic Darwinism. Moreover, Ahriman is the great teacher of all technological and practical ventures in earth-evolution that will not assign validity to anything but external sensory life. These are enterprises that aim purely at a far-spread technology in order that human beings can satisfy the same needs for food and drink that animals satisfy, only in more sophisticated ways.[132]

If we call to mind that it is the metabolic will-system in the human being that is more strongly connected to the body and the earth, we can recognize the terrible danger that menaces humanity through the Ahrimanic beings. Ahriman not only wishes to win over humankind, but the whole earth. Long since, a great battle has ensued on earth that cries out for a decision. This danger can be more clearly experienced in the West than in other regions on earth. But we can likewise sense the possibility of becoming clearly aware of this threat. Seeing this impending danger makes us seek more urgently for ideas and forces that can help and can withstand this danger.

Still, the possibility exists that humanity could lose the faculty of recognizing the helping forces:

> This is the great danger for the age of the consciousness soul. It is the event which still could occur—even prior to the beginning of the third millennium—if human beings would refuse to turn to a spiritual life. We are only a short time away from the beginning of the third millennium. For, as you know, the third millennium begins with the year 2000.[133]

One can have the feeling that Rudolf Steiner spoke in this manner, because he noticed that the people around him harbored the attitude that the third millennium was still far away and that one had plenty of time until its beginning. When Rudolf Steiner uttered these words to his audience, they were 82 years away from the beginning of the new millennium. He considered that to be a short time. Today we are only a few years away from it. We already find ourselves within the boundaries of events that are supposed to happen at the beginning of the third millennium. Every glance at the present tells us this.

Preparation for
Ahriman's Incarnation

The incarnation of Ahriman in America must under no circumstances pass human beings by unawares. As was mentioned before, even the geographic conditions are favorable to Ahriman's intentions, since it is much easier for the double of the West to fetter human beings to the earth. The struggle for recognizing the Ahrimanic activity in the West is a life-or-death question.

Ahriman prepares his incarnation in a variety of ways:

1. Through the materialistically oriented intellectual life of our culture and through "scientific superstition" (meaning that the illusory character of the mechanistic-mathematical world view is not perceived). Coldly abstract knowledge is acquired without genuine interest and is then "conserved" in libraries and such.

2. Through disintegration into groups and parties that fight each other, through intellectually validated party-doctrines that create confusion. Ahriman moreover makes use of what comes from old family disparities and differences between races, tribes, and nations in order to mislead human beings. In all these efforts, the "faith in numbers" comes to his aid, i.e. the manipulation through statistics: "Ahriman can achieve the most through numbers, when they are listed and viewed as means of proof. . . ."[134]

3. Through a one-sided social order that is ruled by purely economic principles and financial thinking, instead of the "threefoldness of the social organism."

If people do not comprehend that they must place the domain of rights and the cultural-spiritual structure over against the economic order—which has originated through economic considerations and the banking systems—then, in such incomprehension, Ahriman will find an essential means for appropriately preparing his incarnation, meaning, the triumph of his incarnation which will definitely take place.[135]

More than anything, Ahriman fears a free cultural-spiritual life.

A free spiritual life is like a form of darkness for the Ahrimanic power. And our regard for such a free life of the spirit will be experienced by Ahriman like a burning fire, a fire of soul, but one that painfully burns.[136]

4. Through materialistic or fundamentalistic interpretations of the Gospels that lead to an illusion, or at best to a sort of hallucinatory vision of the Christ-being, *not to Christ's reality*. Ahriman's activity is even promoted in the setting of denominations or sects (which certainly appeal to "Christ" or "Jesus"), if spiritual scientific insight into comprehension of the Gospels is rejected.

When Ahriman appears in modern civilization in human form, notably those will constitute the beginning of a herd of followers for Ahriman, who belong to religious persuasions and sects today and swear only by the Gospel, while rejecting any true sort of spirit-perception. They are people who do not wish to learn and advance spiritually; they wish to disavow anything that requires spiritual effort for attaining concrete insight. Large numbers of people out of such groups will develop into followers of Ahriman.[137]

Ahriman's incarnation is supposed to occur in the third millennium which is now only a few years away: "In our age today, Lucifer's traces are in a sense less visible, since an incarnation by Ahriman is approaching in the third millennium. . . ."[138] The time when this will happen in the third millennium is not precisely stated. But statements by Rudolf Steiner exist that lead to the assumption that this incarnation will occur *at the beginning* of the next millennium. Several are quoted here: ". . . Before even a segment of the third millennium of our Christian era has gone by, an actual incarnation of Ahriman will take place in the West."[139] His incarnation will come "at a time that is not too far off."[140] On another occasion, Rudolf Steiner speaks of the "imminent incarnation of Ahriman."[141]

Rudolf Steiner called attention to the fact that the mysterious number of the beast that arises out of the earth, 666, has historical significance. He stated that this number had been fulfilled in history twice by now. When the first 666 years after Christ had passed, humanity experienced a first onslaught against spiritual Christianity. It was the time when intellectual thinking, the precursor of today's materialism, came to blossom in Persia in Gondishapur and slowly penetrated the whole Occident.

> The wise men of Gondishapur wanted to accomplish . . . nothing less than to make the human being great and wise for this earth. But by impressing into him this wisdom, they intended to let his soul participate in death, so that he would not be inclined, after passing through the portal of death, to participate in the spiritual life and in subsequent incarnations. Their intention was to cut off his further evolution. They wanted to win him over for themselves, into a completely different world; to conserve him during his

147

earthly life, and to divert him from the purpose for which he is on earth, namely, from all he has to learn in a slow, gradual development, a development that will lead to spirit-self, life-spirit, and spirit-man.[142]

Seen from a religious standpoint, through Arabism, Islam spread during this time. It developed a view of the godhead fundamentally differing from that of Christianity. It renounces the Trinity of Father, Son, and Holy Spirit; it views Christ Jesus merely as man, not the cosmic divine being that incarnated in Jesus. The Islamic religion only knows the one, all-encompassing god. Mohammed, as well as Jesus, are just the human prophets of Allah, a view that prevails today among segments of Protestant Christians.

A second, fiercer attack occurred in 1332, hence two-times 666. Some time earlier, Philip IV of France had imprisoned the Templars, knights in whom the feeling of a new, deeper, and more spiritual Christianity had come to life. The king had seized their treasures of gold and had them tortured again and again in order to extract from their turbulently whipped-up soul-forces confessions of guilt while their consciousness was dimmed, confessions that they later recanted when in their normal state of mind. He had many of them burned at the stake. Through the possession of tremendous gold treasures that evoked an immoderate sense of power in the king and through the eerie experiences of the tortures, something erupted in him of the spirit of the ancient Ahrimanic-Mexican mysteries:

And so it could come to pass that certain insights arose in the soul of Philip IV, the Handsome, insights of a lower sort, of that form of perception we saw blazing up in the coarsest, most horrible way in the Mexican mysteries. Philip IV, the Handsome, realized what one can accomplish if one destroys life in the

148

appropriate manner in the world, even though in a different way from the Mexican initiates and not in such a direct, but an indirect way. As if out of deeply unconscious motives, he found the means to incorporate unconscious impulses into humanity's evolution through the killing of men. He needed his victims for this.[143]

One cannot help but ask what happened from 1933 to 1945 in Central Europe, when Hitler had five to six million people murdered. This is how, in faraway Mexico, an Ahrimanic spirit could be trained and become effective centuries later. The actions of Philip IV led to the destruction of the Order of the Templars, and with it, to one of the most mysterious events in history. Following their death, the Templars turned into the strongest champions of a new cosmic Christianity which they had not been able to realize then, for the time had not yet come. This is something that Anthroposophy wishes to realize today.

If we try to understand the most powerful attack presently being readied in the age of the development of the consciousness soul, an age in which the ego must be recognized and taken hold of in its true nature, we have to remember that the 666 years are being fulfilled for the third time, namely, in 1998. With that, we arrive at the end of the century and the beginning of the third millennium. Then, as mentioned earlier, the Asuras will intrude into the consciousness soul. The Asuras are Ahrimanic beings, but stand on a higher level than the fallen angels or retarded archangel-beings. They were Archai-beings, hence, possess tremendous power. This distinguishes them from other Ahrimanic beings. Their battle is aimed directly against the human ego. They want to rob the ego of its power and thus chain the human being to the earth. With that, he would be completely thrown off the track of his evolution. It is not in any way an exaggeration to depict this greatest onslaught of the Ahrimanic-Asuric beings as the decisive conflict with the Christ-forces on earth. It will be a decisive battle for the direction that humanity will pursue. Although we do not know the precise time of Ahriman's incarnation in the West, we will find ourselves in the year 2000 (1998) at the *peak of the preparations* that Ahriman has been carrying out for several centuries. We are already standing in the midst of the decisive event—actually, we have been in it since the beginning of the Michael-reign in 1879.

In *Menschenwerden, Weltenseele und Weltengeist* (Human Evolution, World Soul, and Cosmic Spirit), Rudolf Steiner shows that, if humanity remains stuck in materialism, all things spiritual that are trying to develop in human soul-depths turn into their opposites. They will then infuse the intensification and brutalization of urges, instincts, and the destructive powers of the soul. A terrible egoism will unfold in human souls. A dreadful hardening of the ego will take place. This has to be said, for these are not theoretic thoughts, they occur all around us: "If matters are allowed to continue . . . we will face the war of all against all at the end of the 20th century."[144] In this sense, we should pay attention to the never-ending wars, the racial confrontations, the battle waged by political, even religious groups, with bombs, innocent hostages, and deeds of violence in which women participate increasingly as well. Criminality is constantly on the rise in America. All this continues to evolve rapidly. And so we must take Rudolf Steiner's words seriously when he says that a war of all against all will be fully raging at the end of the century. But this likewise shows that something most decisive has to ensue at the end of the century on the part of the good spiritual powers, for otherwise the fate of humanity would already have been decided.

AHRIMAN AND THE SPIRITS OF FORM

After the first 666 years of our Christian era had passed, intellectual thinking initially awoke, which later-on brought materialism. Ahriman's struggle was directed against thinking and herewith against the individual bearers of thinking, the individual human beings. When the second 666 years were nearly over, Ahriman waged his battle against the community of the Templars. He not only took hold of individuals but tried to destroy communities of human beings. To this purpose he intervened in the experience and feeling of men who annihilated the Templars. While approaching the end of the third 666 years, he wages battle against humanity, against human will, against the ego. With this, he attacks the very essence of what gives meaning to the earth's and humankind's evolution. The struggle for the earth has been launched. Ahriman now wishes to subjugate her. Earth is to follow in his direction. Since the beginning of the Michael-reign in 1879, we can observe how this intent to make himself master of the earth is mirrored in the great social and political movements. The contrast between Russia and America basically has to do with domination of the earth. In Adolf Hitler's National Socialism, this will became especially apparent. Early on, in the days of the Roman Empire, a first attempt was made to transfer world-leadership to one nation. It failed. Along with Asuric expansion of power, Ahriman's desire is to extinguish anything that opposes his will.

We recall that on every hierarchical level beings remain behind:

You can readily imagine that there are beings, who, during the Moon evolution, should have ascended to the level of Revelations or Powers (Exusiai), but only reached the stage of the Primal Forces (Archai). These Archai differ from those hierarchical beings who, in the regular course of evolution, rose to the Archai-level. There exist therefore Archai who are in fact camouflaged Exusiai on earth.[145]

Exusiai are Spirits of Form, the Elohim who created the earth. Yahweh, who at the beginning guided actual earth-evolution, while the other Elohim held back, was one of them. Other beings, who were supposed to attain to this stage, fell short of it and therefore stand between Archai-beings and Spirits of Form. They do work as Archai-beings:

> . . . among them—albeit only for those who view this from a spiritual scientific viewpoint—belongs the being who is rightfully called "Satan," Satan, the false prince of this world, for the true one is a "Power," Yahweh or Jehova. The false one belongs to the order of the Primal Forces. He expresses himself by constantly causing confusion for the Time Spirit among human beings, bringing people to the point of constantly contradicting the Spirit of the Age.[146]

He is the false prince "of our earth who makes the claim that he is the one who in fact guides and leads humankind."[147]

The Spirits of Form are beings who dwell in the eighth sphere. Human beings dwell in the fourth sphere. Above us are three more spheres; they belong to us inasmuch as they represent humanity's future. Beyond it is the eighth sphere: "When you now look at this eighth sphere, in it dwell not only our divine spirits of creation but likewise the Ahrimanic beings."[148] We thus encounter Ahriman as an Archai-being, endowed with a power that approaches that of the Spirits of Form. He is therefore a dangerous opponent for Michael and those who serve him. Ahriman is a spirit that has the power to take up the battle for the earth. We do not know exactly when the incarnation will take place; but when we observe the outer events, it is obvious that, at the turn of the century, we will enter into a new and decisive state of human evolution. The old world order will come completely to an end. In all areas of cultural life, a tough, decisive battle between Christianized and un-Christianized thinking will run its course. Following these mighty controversies, we will find ourselves in a world that in no way will resemble today's world.

Unusual parallel events exist from which we may be able to decipher something. When, during His descent from cosmic heights, Christ appeared on the Sun in the middle of the Atlantean Age, the cast-down dragon-spirits took up their battle against the Christ-impulse from the earth. Shortly before the Mystery of Golgotha occurred in Palestine, the black magician in Mexico tried to acquire the power to undo the effect of this event. In the 15th and 16th centuries, Michael established a supersensible school in the spiritual world in which he gathered all human, subhuman, and higher spiritual beings who belonged with him. He prepared them for the decisive events at the beginning of the third millennium. Ahriman likewise founded a school. In it, he brought together all those belonging to him in order to ready them for his coming:

> While Michael schooled his hosts above, directly under the surface of the earth a sort of subterranean Ahrimanic school was instituted.[149]

When, in 1879, Michael began his reign of time in order to prepare the way for Christ, the Ahrimanic beings on earth were able to bring materialism to a culmination. The effect of this will maintain and continue materialism for a long time yet. Christ experienced His second Golgotha, because the dead, who had imbued themselves with materialism, had become so powerful that they could extinguish the Christ-consciousness in the ether-world.

Rudolf Steiner told of another parallel event, perhaps the most significant one for our age. He describes how Ahriman will emerge as an author of books. Initially through Nietzsche, he was able to write a few books, but that was merely a beginning. With brilliant intelligence, by means of certain human beings, he himself will write books on all topics of science and the social and cultural life, in order to direct humans toward his goals. He will train people living even now on earth, to the end that he can use them later-on as his instruments. Rudolf Steiner states that those working on earth for the Michaelic intelligence must develop alertness

in confronting the brilliant, dazzling activity by Ahriman as an author, work that will be effective throughout the whole 20th century. He will write these works at the strangest locations, but they will be available, and he will develop his following of pupils.[150]

And then Rudolf Steiner makes a surprising comment:

Any number of phenomena appear already in our time that are intended to train human souls subconsciously so they will reincarnate quickly and turn into tools for Ahriman as an author.[151]

This means that not only those persons will reincarnate who belong to the Michael stream, but likewise people from Ahriman's stream: "This will be the situation that humanity will confront at the end of the century."[152]

Nothing else can demonstrate more clearly how Ahriman views the turn of the century and how he prepares himself for this event. He even has the power to bring his pupils down to earth for this battle. Ahriman knows what will be involved. Rudolf Steiner describes the task of the Anthroposophical Society and all its daughter-movements as follows:

> Two things will be important in coming human developments. To the extent that it is possible, the effort will have to be made to continue in the earthly domain with the cultivation of what Michael once taught the predestined souls in supersensible schools; to be reverent in regard to these insights within the Anthroposophical Society and to instruct those, who subsequently will incarnate, in these insights until the end of the 20th century will be upon us.[153]

Ahriman's Undertakings
in The Life After Death

In order to understand better what Ahriman tries to achieve through his incarnation on earth, we have to take a look at the life after death of those people who on earth thought and felt only along materialistic lines:

> Materialistic thoughts prevail here on earth. In the spiritual world, as a karma resulting from such thoughts, materialistic consequence prevails, that is, the spiritual corporeality of the dead becomes infused with earthward leanings.[154]

What does it mean "to become infused with earthward leanings"? When, during life on earth, the etheric body engages in too close a union with the physical body, it loses its own power and formative force and assumes the structuring order of the physical body. It rigidifies and solidifies more and more. That is an essential goal for the Ahrimanic powers. It is also the aim of the double in us. People in this way chain themselves to the forces of the earth. After death, when the physical body has been laid aside, the etheric body cannot dissolve, because the aftereffects of the structural order of the earthly body, its solidity and densification still persist. Due to that, such persons cannot free themselves from the earth's ether-surroundings in order to ascend to higher spheres of existence. For a long time, they remain bound to earth and must serve Ahriman.

In the Post-Atlantean Age, not only the spiritual side of earth-existence turned increasingly dark for human beings—

this began as early as the Fall—but likewise life after death, even up to the Greek Cultural Epoch. At that time, the world after death had darkened so much that a Greek wanted rather to be a beggar on earth than a king in the realm of shades. During the three days between His death and resurrection, Christ remained in the underworld, in "hell," with the dead who no longer could raise themselves up from the earth to the spirit world. Christ placed Ahriman, who had acquired great power in this kingdom, into fetters, and thus opened the portal to the divine world for the dead, but only for those humans who began to fill themselves with the Christ-impulse:

> Outside the forces that stream out from the Christ-mystery, there will be less and less protection in the world against the influence of Ahriman. In a certain sense, our age—and many phenomena proclaim this—draws closer to such Ahrimanic influences.[155]

This has consequences in the life after death: the human being remains tied to earth for a long time and thus causes destructive forces to flow into the physical world.

One important insight is to see through Ahriman's intention of trying to prepare human beings on earth in such a way that, following death, they have to remain for a time in his domain. Still, again and again, they can free themselves from Ahriman's realm, because karma and reincarnation lead them further through life after death, albeit unconsciously for them, until they begin to descend again to earth. Ahriman, on the other hand, would really like to hold human beings back forever in his sphere of action. Up until now he has not succeeded. One step in this direction is the following: there are factions in the West that would like to secure the world domination for the English-speaking nations. The language and the forms of thought in these factions gain significance and power in the following way:

> In our materialistic age today, thinking is contained, as it were, in language for a great many people. In today's materialistic age, people hardly think in thoughts, but very decidedly in a language, in words. . . . After death, however, the task is to become free of all verbal designations.[156]

Already while still on the earth, one has to become free of words, if one wishes to arrive at actual ideas.

> I have often shown you how, by looking at something from all sides and using any number of different words, you must try to free yourselves of the word in order to arrive at the concept. Spiritual science emancipates us in a sense from language. It does so to the fullest extent. And by so doing, it brings us into the sphere we have in common with the dead.[157]

After death, in order to free themselves from the folk-bound earthly language and the manner of thinking conditioned by it, human beings must seek for a connection with the archangels. In that way, the dead attain to the possibility of awakening in a consciousness common to all humanity. But in those factions in the West, people do not think based on humanity. They think based on their group-interest. And if one works based on interests and goals of narrowly defined groups, this has consequences in life after death:

> Through what is envisioned in such groups, it becomes possible for individuals to find their way into the spiritual world and be pervaded by the Hierarchy

of the Angels, but not to ascend to the Hierarchy of the Archangels. In a way, the aim is to dismiss the Archangels from humanity's evolution.[158]

We have to remember: "Emancipation from language is intimately connected with growing into the substantiality of the Archangels."[159] Now, in life after death, the dead cannot be "nourished" solely by the Angels. They have to have a substitute for the legitimate Archangels who are sidestepped. "And they do receive an equivalent, . . . they are imbued by something that derives from those Archai who have remained behind on the archangelic level."[160] Instead of being pervaded by the legitimate Archangels, these dead are infiltrated by other beings, beings who likewise stand on the archangelic level but are retarded Archai-beings: "This means that the dead are in the most drastic sense Ahrimanically infested."[161] Something quite uncommon has been achieved in their case: "Ahrimanic immortality has been attained for them."[162]

Hearing such a description, one has to consider that occult groups in the West pursue various goals. Here, Rudolf Steiner speaks of *one* group, but perhaps an important one:

> You might say: How could people be foolish enough to plan methodically to detach themselves from normal evolution and to enter into quite another spiritual development? Yet, this is a shortsighted judgment, one that does not consider at all that, due to certain impulses, people might long to seek immortality in worlds quite other than those we designate as the normal ones. . . . It is incomprehensible . . . when people . . . persuade themselves: We no longer wish to have Christ as the guide, Christ who is indeed the guide through this normal world. We wish to have a different leader; we want to be in opposition to this normal world.[163]

If one ponders these thoughts for a while, one realizes that there are people who, through these experiences after death, drop out of the evolution led by the good gods and thereafter pursue different paths. Ahriman tries to separate earthly human beings from their primal creator-gods. In this way, he would win them over to his own planet, a planet he plans to form when the end of the world comes. Ahriman, who in many regards usurped for himself what the Yahweh-deity did rightfully, continues this in his direction, uniting with the Ancient Moon-forces:

> A time will come when those who cling to materialistic reason will unite with Moon-powers. Together with the moon, they will surround the earth, when it has become a slag-heap, a corpse. For these beings, these humans, who insist on connecting themselves with the materialistic intellect, want nothing else but to hold on to the earth's life, to remain united with the life of the earth. They do not wish to arise in the proper way from the earth's corpse to what will then be the soul-spiritual side of the earth.[164]

Here, we are confronted by two world perspectives, two evolutionary possibilities. With deep consternation, we confront an infinite tragedy in human evolution: humanity will divide and go their separate ways! There are those who will go with the dying earth, with the earth's corpse, and sink down by one level. The others will go on with the true spiritual earth in order to reach a higher level of human development. Ahriman prepares the former. Along with his appearance on earth, it will become apocalyptic reality: speaking pictorially, one part of humanity will bear on their forehead the sign of the beast; the other part will bear on their forehead the sign of God.

Ahriman's Incarnation
and its Goals

A certain human being will be made ready who will, at the right moment, make room in his earthly body for Ahriman, so that herewith Ahriman's activity on earth can begin. The fact that Ahriman was able to be active in a fair number of people as an author in all areas of knowledge, art, the social and religious life is merely an introduction to his actual incarnation. Then he himself will be active "in the flesh" in a very differentiated way. A most important and almost unexpected way of functioning is described by Rudolf Steiner as follows:

> When Ahriman has incarnated at the right moment in the Western world, he will institute a great occult school. In this occult school, the most remarkable magical feats will be produced, and what can otherwise only be attained by great effort will be poured out over humankind.[165]

He will be able to transmit supersensible wisdom to his students, which they will be able to receive without having to change their thinking. Ahriman wishes to preserve the thinking that exists today. Rudolf Steiner adds:

> We should not placidly imagine that, when Ahriman descends, he will be a sort of devilish trickster who plays practical jokes on human beings. Oh no, all those easygoing folks, who say today that they do not wish to know anything of spiritual science, would succumb to his magic, for in the most grandiose way possible he will be capable of turning human beings . . . into clairvoyants.[166]

If, on the one hand, he makes every effort as an author to preserve today's knowledge and thinking, why does he want to make human beings clairvoyant? It goes without saying that Ahriman possesses clear insight into all that tries to develop in humanity, particularly from the spiritual aspect. And so he knows that clairvoyant faculties will arise in humanity in the normal course of evolution. He likewise knows that these faculties will be directed toward the etherically appearing Christ. These faculties are now becoming more and more pronounced. Ahriman has to reckon with that. Indeed, the time will come when everything will pass over into the spiritual dimension. He wants to shape that process to suit his own purposes. When he causes human beings to become clairvoyant without their having to change themselves, can he divert the perception of Christ's etheric appearance? The clairvoyance that he plans to bring will be fundamentally different from what will develop through spiritual science. In the Ahrimanically produced clairvoyance, each person will have his or her own subjective visions, visions that do not coincide with those of others:

> People would . . . only engage in quarrels and strife. . . . But in the end they would be quite content with their visions.[167]

How would Ahrimanic clairvoyance be structured? If human beings remain as they are, and if they need not transform present intellectual thinking nor their life of feeling and passions, they will lose the ancient guiding forces of the Yahweh-deity that work in a regulatory way. Ahriman can then grab hold of the sphere of instincts and urges and change it into clairvoyant imaginations.

Then something comes about that resembles the description Rudolf Steiner gives in "The Tree of Life and the Tree of Knowledge of Good and Evil:"

> This whole world of instincts, which is really an egotistical domain, one that belongs only to the human being, can emancipate itself, as it were, from the Yahweh-deity that dwells within it. Then its influences rise up. Unconsciously, without the person being aware of them, they push their way through and infest the conceptual realm with their imaginations. People become clairvoyant, as it is often called, they have visions. They experience everything contained in their sphere of instincts as imaginations. In truth, they actually experience only their world of passions; these confront such persons as an imaginative world. But since it is really the cosmos that indwells us in veiled form in our whole world of instincts, the imaginations that rise like a mist out of human passions and urges simulate a whole cosmos to people.[168]

Since we all have different instincts and urges, each one of us dwells in his or her own private, enclosed existence. We experience ourselves, not the true spiritual world. We are supposed to become conscious of our drives and instincts which are of will-like nature, but we should do so with clear, spiritual *thoughts*, else they billow and steam upward and overpower our spiritual striving.

> This is what is important: The future wisdom that is of a clairvoyant nature must once more be taken away from Ahriman. One might say: It is only *one* book, not two wisdoms—*one* book. And the point is whether Ahriman has the book, or Christ. Christ cannot have it without humanity fighting for it. And we can only fight for it by telling ourselves that, by the

165

time Ahriman appears on earth, we must have acquired this content of spiritual wisdom through our own efforts.[169]

In that way, we can completely incorporate this "book" of world-wisdom, which John, the writer of the Apocalypse, received from the "mighty angel" and ate.

It would be the worst advice that one could give human beings, if one told them: Just remain as you are! Ahriman will make all of you clairvoyant, if you so desire. And you will desire it, for Ahriman will have great power. But the result of this would be that the kingdom of Ahriman would be established on earth[170]

Ahriman wishes to become ruler of the earth, the double would like to become master of human evolution. Rudolf Steiner speaks of this as follows:

If the Mystery of Golgotha had not taken place, if Christ had not gone through the Mystery of Golgotha, then, on earth, these doubles would long since have successfully acquired the possibility of remaining within human beings, when the latter are karmically destined to meet death. The doubles would then have gained victory over human evolution; they would have become the rulers of human evolution on earth.[171]

Rudolf Steiner then adds:

It is of tremendous significance to obtain insight into these connections between Christ's passing through the Mystery of Golgotha and those beings who wish to conquer death in human nature, death which, *as yet, in the present time,* they cannot tolerate.[172]

Not yet today, but they are trying to tolerate it! Until now, the Mystery of Golgotha has prevented this. The double lives in the unconscious realm, as was outlined. It is connected to a person through the body. In passing through the Event on Golgotha, Christ created the new body, the resurrection body, the phantom. After death, we can maintain our I-consciousness only through this new body and acquire immortality for ourselves. We can know of ourselves and can thus remain united with the earth *spiritually*. Immortality is not simply a continuation of life after death. It is a matter of having consciousness of self. And one can only have that if one can develop a spirit-body after death.

Is it the goal of the doubles to acquire a sort of Ahrimanic spirit-body in and through human beings, so that they can yet turn themselves into the rulers of the earth? In *Man and the World of Stars* Rudolf Steiner describes a strange fact. He speaks of Moon, Venus, and Mercury beings who unlawfully dwell on earth:

> These beings are identical to those whom I have counted among the Ahrimanic beings in other lectures. They have the task of confining the human being to the earth as much as possible.[173]

Rudolf Steiner mentions that the earth will eventually dissolve and pass over into the Jupiter condition:

> This is what these beings try to prevent. Above all, they wish to prevent human beings, along with the earth, from completing their development in the regular way and then to evolve in a normal manner into the Jupiter condition. They want to conserve earth's existence. . . .[174]

They really want to rob the human being of his future. They aim for a different earth evolution and a different human evolution on the preserved earth. It is not an easy task to separate the human being from his intended higher development. But they know how they can try it:

> These Moon, Venus, and Mercury beings, who wrongfully dwell on the earth, presently try to give human beings an etheric body fashioned out of the earth's ether during each period of sleep. They are almost never successful. In rare cases, of which I will speak another time, they were successful, but still they almost never are.[175]

The normal ether body is condensed out of the cosmic world-ether. These Ahrimanic beings wish to form an ether body out of the earth's ether. This is the great difference. Such an etheric body would no longer contain cosmic wisdom, only earthly wisdom, no cosmic thinking, but only earthly thinking. Through such an ether body one would be fettered to the earth and be cut off from the cosmos. Furthermore, he says:

> If such an Ahrimanic being would actually be successful in installing a whole ether body in a person step by step . . . after death, when human beings are in their ether body, such a person would be able to survive in his/her etheric body. Normally, the etheric body dissolves within a few days [after death]. But such people would be able to survive in their etheric body; an etheric human race would eventually come into being. This is what is intended from this side of the spiritual world. Earth could thereby be preserved. In fact, within the solid and fluid earth-structure, we have such a horde of beings who would like to turn humanity gradually—by the end of the earth—into ghosts, etheric ghosts, so that the goal, the normal goal of earth-evolution, could not be reached.[176]

After their death, people would remain imprisoned in a new etheric body formed out of earth's ether, for this etheric body would not dissolve. They would be held fast to the earth's ether-realm. Such people would be unable to ascend to cosmic heights; they would remain chained forever to earth as egoless soul beings. Rudolf Steiner called this process "the turning of the spiritual corporeality of the dead into a thing of the earth."

In order to become better acquainted with a certain religious movement active in America, I attended an introduction to their religious body of thoughts. Part of it consisted of watching two movies. One film dealt with life after death. You saw the departed as man and wife, just as they had lived on earth, a man as a man, a woman as a woman. They had the same earthly bodies as on earth, even wore the same suits and dresses. They talked and enjoyed themselves just as they had on earth. These people take along with them their purely materialistic images of life after death. They feel comfortable in an atmosphere where they can live in bodies that are just like their bodies on earth. They develop no need to strive beyond this sphere. Now, this is connected with another and most important impulse of Ahriman's. We must remember that the task of the Lucifer-incarnation was to produce thinking on earth by means of creating a physical-corporeal organ, the brain. Lucifer was the first being incarnated on earth that could activate this brain-thinking. Today, Ahriman poses himself the opposite task. He tries to make thinking independent of the physical brain. Rudolf Steiner explains that Ahriman has the desire to preserve the thinking that is intellectually active on earth, something one can see from the many libraries that preserve earthly knowledge in millions of books, and with that, the form of present-day thinking.

This thinking, which Ahriman not only tries to preserve in physical earth life, but wants to turn into the only source of knowledge, is furthermore not supposed to dissolve after death together with the human being's etheric body. It is supposed to go on living independent of the brain. This would give Ahriman a power he has not possessed up to now. We have to be clear on this: the etheric body is a living body of thoughts. But it can lose its living energy and wither. Pure brain thinking then comes about:

> The substance that lives in the etheric body has been woven into the human being out of the etheric nature of the cosmos. It can never separate completely from the cosmos. Cosmic-etheric processes continue into the human organization; their inner human continuation is our ether-organism. That is why, at the moment when self-consciousness arises after death in our etheric organism, this consciousness begins right away to change into a cosmic consciousness. In the very same way we feel our ether-organism as something that is within our own being, we feel the ether of the cosmos. In reality, however, this means that within a very short time the etheric body dissolves in the cosmic ether.[177]

Dissolution of the etheric body implies the transformation of earthly consciousness into cosmic consciousness and moreover ascent to the further cosmic evolution of the human being.

Anthroposophy's innermost task, at the present time, is to enliven the brain-bound thinking which has turned intellectual and arid, so that it becomes etherized and spiritualized. Thus, it gradually will be free and independent of the brain. It becomes body-free thinking that can open itself to the cosmos. The Ahrimanic "resurrection body," if one dares call it that, likewise gives the human being thought-filled conscious-ness after death. It gives human beings "eternal life," but only in connection with the preserved earth. Christ wishes to create a new spiritual earth from the old earth, namely, earth's Jupiter-state. Ahriman wishes to preserve, condense, and harden the old earth, together with its etheric sheath, in order to turn it into a dwelling place for his beings, into a new planet of his own. He wants to preserve intellectual thinking through a "condensed ether-body" for the life after death, even if a physical brain is no longer there.

As was mentioned earlier, Rudolf Steiner refers to certain occult societies that serve Ahriman's purposes on earth. Typically, ancient magic rituals are conducted in them, rituals that link participants together even beyond death. These participants not only pursue their goals here on earth, but try to remain actively involved in them even after death:

> The other point is that these people, who join the circles of certain magic, ceremonial societies, secure for themselves a power that extends beyond death, an Ahrimanic immortality, as it were. And this is the motivating thought in the case of a large number of such people. . . . In a sense, the society they have joined is like a guarantor that the powers they have will live beyond death, powers that actually should last only until their physical death. And this thought lives in more people today than you would imagine, the thought of securing an Ahrimanic immortality— the Ahrimanic immortality that consists not only of working as a single, individual human being, but as an instrument of a society such as I have character-ized earlier.[178]

What is it that happens in an ancient magic-cultic ritual? For the duration of the ritual, retarded angels influence and

work on the astral, etheric, and physical bodies of the participants, bypassing their consciousness, in order to change these
people to suit their purposes. Such persons are then no longer
able to harbor in themselves their eternal individuality that
passes through the incarnations; instead, they seek for
Ahrimanic immortality. The goal of earth's preservation is
added to Ahrimanic immortality. Concerning this, Rudolf
Steiner says:

> When we are born, we have gathered together a
> new will, but thought detaches itself and finds the
> head; the will takes over the remainder of the body.
> While we live on earth, a constant alternating activity
> exists between will and thought. Will takes hold of
> thought. We in turn must carry this combination of
> will and thought through death. Ahriman would like
> to prevent our doing so. He would like will to remain
> by itself; only thought should be particularly devel-
> oped in us. We would lose our individuality, if at last
> it really came to what Ahriman actually intends. We
> would completely lose our individuality. We would
> arrive at the moment of death with an almost exag-
> gerated, instinctively developed form of thought. But
> we human beings could not hold on to such thought.
> Ahriman could usurp and fit it into the remaining
> world so that such thought would then continue its
> effects in the rest of the world. This is in fact the fate
> that threatens humanity, if we continue with present-
> day materialism. The Ahrimanic powers would
> become so powerful that Ahriman could rob human
> beings of their thoughts and then incorporate them
> into the earth insofar as their effectiveness is con-
> cerned, so that earth, which actually should come to
> an end, remains consolidated. Ahriman aims toward
> ... earth remaining as earth. Ahriman works against
> the saying, "Heaven and earth will pass away but my
> words will not pass away" [Matt. 25:35]. He would

like these words to be cast aside and for heaven and earth to remain as they are.[179]

On the one hand, Ahriman would like thinking without will in order to conquer it. On the other hand, he would like to give the human being an etheric body that is woven exclusively out of earth-ether, not out of cosmic ether which leads him upward to cosmic consciousness. In this way, Ahriman creates a thinking without an "I". He can grab hold of such thinking and use it for his own purposes. In its hardening strength, he leads it into the earth in order to consolidate the latter.

In the coming Ahriman-incarnation, much will become possible that Ahriman or those following him have envisioned for a long time, but were not able to attain. As a being incarnated in an earthly body, he will succeed in making earth-thinking independent of the human brain so that human beings can take it along into the world after death. Throughout the centuries, Ahriman has aspired to this and, by his own efforts, it will become partially possible for him. Human beings who follow in his direction are supposed to become capable of maintaining their thinking after death, and not only their thinking capacity, but their memory. They are able to take along the knowledge they worked to attain, and to elaborate on it. Then, they will be in a position to preserve their earthly consciousness of self, even if their physical body has fallen away. It will not be a consciousness of their actual ego-being but a limited earth-ether-consciousness. These human beings will not be able to unfold a free "I", but instead will be consciously thinking group-beings of sorts, tools of Ahriman. They will become much more powerful than the dead heretofore in influencing human beings on earth and in producing world-destructive forces. Through the unlawfully active Moon, Venus, and Mercury beings on earth, Ahriman will furthermore succeed in implanting into human beings a new etheric body consisting merely of earth-ether. This etheric body will be the bearer of will-devoid earth-thinking that is taken along [in death], the bearer of memory and a new self-awareness after death. All this will make it possible for the doubles to remain in human beings when they cross the threshold of death. No longer will the doubles be threatened with dissolution of their consciousness; they will not be torn away into a direction that could prove to be dangerous for them through the transformation of earth-consciousness after death into cosmic consciousness. The doubles can only remain in an etheric body that has turned earthly, and in earthly thinking. They can then remain united with the earth and its forces and strengthen the dead in their earth-oriented thinking and doings.

Human beings who play a leading role in the pursuit of Ahriman's goals on earth, for example, those who are involved in occult groups with ancient cults, will be the first to attain for themselves Ahrimanic immortality. With heightened consciousness, they will be able to continue pursuing their earthly goals beyond death. Here, we have to take into consideration that higher development will exist even in Ahriman's kingdom: unconscious instruments of Ahriman, more consciously cooperating human beings, Angels, Archangels, Archai, and Ahriman as a fallen Spirit of Form. Initiated heralds of Ahriman, like the black magician in Mexico, will attain the possibility of rising above the earth's sphere to worlds where they hope to discover the insights of how the cosmic Christ-wisdom can be banished from the earth and to darken the earth so far that the cosmic light in it will be extinguished. This way they would be able to assume leadership over earth-evolution. The difficulty of the initiates of black magic was that, by producing the cold, heartless thinking in themselves through the slaying of life, they were exposed so powerfully to the earth's forces of gravity that they no longer could rise to cosmic heights on their own. They had to kill human beings in order to be carried up to the desired worlds in the souls of the sacrificed persons who were fleeing the earth in shock. These initiates could only undertake such a flight to the heights from time to time. This was why they aspired to a continuous initiation. This will become possible for Ahriman through his earthly incarnation and the forces that will thereby greatly increase in him. For this to happen, it is necessary for Ahriman to separate human and spirit-beings, who are linked to him, from their proper hierarchy in order to form his own.

This will be attained through those Archangels who are actually retarded Archai. Something they could not accomplish heretofore will become possible for them, namely, to cut human beings off completely from their rightful Archangels. These could have bestowed *a consciousness, an awareness of humanity* on human beings that would have allowed them to remain united with their proper hierarchy. Through the development of such a consciousness, human beings would have been liberated from earthly restraints, from a language of a specific ethnic group, folk and blood communities. The Ahrimanic Archangels prevent this. Human beings must then follow Ahriman's path. Through their newly acquired power, Ahriman will succeed in the aspirations he has had ever since Roman times, namely, to have a new world empire spring up. This empire will acquire world domination through rigidly executed inner and outer centralism. Beyond that, it will make any free self-development on earth impossible. Ahriman hopes that, in this way, he will finally extinguish cosmic wisdom or spiritual science on earth. Through new insights, discoveries, and breakthroughs, through manipulations involving the human body, Ahriman will be successful in attaining decisive influence over the shaping of human souls. In the technological field, he will institute further accomplishments in the direction of strengthening "mechanistic" or materialistic occultism. Through his incarnation, Ahriman will lay the foundation stone for a new planet. With that, the battle for the earth will enter a decisive phase.

In view of what will develop, one might easily lose courage. But we should acquire clear-sighted, fearless awareness for the dangers that now threaten humanity, else we do not perceive how difficult the conflicts will be. Here, I would like to repeat a statement by Rudolf Steiner that can uplift us:

> One task of human beings for the impending development of civilization will be to meet the Ahriman incarnation in such full awareness that this incarnation can serve . . . a higher . . . spiritual development.[180]

It is possible to transform Ahriman's activities prior to, during, and following his incarnation on earth in such a way that it *can* serve the higher development of humanity!

In all this, we clearly have to recognize the spiritual power of cosmic wisdom. When observing the events of the present, one can be fooled and underestimate the former. This is why it is beneficial to hear Rudolf Steiner on this subject:

> What has been stated by initiates in all ages is true: When human beings are steeped in the effects of spiritual wisdom, this is a great horror of darkness for the Ahrimanic beings, a consuming fire. The Ahrimanic Angels feel comfortable dwelling in human heads today that are filled with Ahrimanic science.

On the other hand, those heads that are imbued with spiritual wisdom are experienced by the Ahrimanic Angels like a consuming fire, a great horror of darkness. We should sense the deep seriousness of this and feel that imbuing ourselves with spiritual wisdom means moving through this world in such a manner that we establish a proper relationship to the Ahrimanic powers. Through what we ourselves do, we erect what has to be present, namely, that for the good of the world we erect the site of the consuming fire of sacrifice, the site where the horror of darkness rays over the destructive Ahrimanic element.[181]

Such sites are a necessity, particularly in the West.

TURN OF THE CENTURY – TURN OF THE MILLENNIUM

The significance of the imminent turn of the century is that, at the same time, it is the turn of the millennium. We leave the second millennium of Christian evolution and enter the third. In repeating the pre-Christian times, we thus enter the age of Abraham, an age that, according to Rudolf Steiner, is to bring humanity great things. And this millennium will immediately be introduced by the most decisive struggle that has ever been waged between humankind and the opposing powers. If understood spiritually, even the Apocalypse speaks of this turning point. According to the description by Rudolf Steiner in *The Apocalypse of St. John*, mighty epochs of time are described in the seven letters, seven seals, seven trumpets and seven bowls of wrath.[182] Even as the seven tones of the octave (the eighth is only a repetition of the first tone on the higher level) are always the same in the lower or higher pitch, so the trumpets, for example, apply to larger but also smaller time periods. This means that the age of the fifth trumpet would begin at the end of the 17th century, the sixth would span the time from 1841 to the year 2000, and the seventh would start with the beginning of the new millennium. These last three trumpets, the fifth, sixth, and seventh, are also called the three "woes." Thus, we find ourselves in the second "woe" and are nearing the third.

Earlier, from the 15th to the 18th century, the celestial school in the spiritual worlds was held, the school in which Michael introduced his pupils to the cosmic Christ-permeated world-wisdom. This he did in preparation for the coming decisive conflict with the Ahrimanic powers:

> It was a tremendous process, something that caused the Ahrimanic demons on earth profound discomfort, especially in the 15th, 16th, 17th, and all the way into the 18th century. . . .[183]

Michael in his school lifted the spiritual interrelationships, that earlier had only been accessible to the intellectual and sentient soul, "into intelligent consciousness, namely the consciousness soul" for his pupils. Simultaneously, Ahriman established a spiritual counter-school in the sphere directly under the surface of the earth. It served the intensive preparation of his incarnation on earth and the events at the end of the 20th century. This lasted into the 18th century. With that begins the time of the three woes; there begin the terrestrial effects of what Ahriman prepared in his subterranean school. The second call of woe starts with the before-mentioned events around 1840. Everywhere, Ahriman sowed the seeds that are intended to germinate for him at the end of our century. Michael establishes his time-reign in order to hold the powers of darkness in check. During the period of the second woe, the two world wars have completely altered the face of the earth. In a few years, the third woe begins, the culmination of the spirit-battle that will decide the direction in which humanity will continue. This will not be an easy time. It will be a hard time, a time of "woe."

When Rudolf Steiner spoke for the first time about the events around the turn of the century, he told his listeners that all those who belong to the Michael-stream would reincarnate, meaning those who were already incarnated in the 20th century; along with them, the Platonists would appear, who had remained in the spiritual world for a long time; they would all incarnate in order to participate in the decisive battle which would then take place. At that time, in the listeners the realization dawned that it would not be our time, as important as it is, that will be the decisive one but the period that begins with the turn of the century. Our time, the time from 1841 to the year 2000, the age of the sixth trumpet, brought the beginning of the Michael-rule and Anthroposophy, the revelation of the mysteries of the divine-spiritual worlds. With that it brought to those who accepted it, a completely new view of the world and human being. Yet, people also realized that the time that was then to follow will be the most important one for humanity. It will bring us the toughest battle with Ahriman, but, on the other hand, the possibility of becoming cognizant of the etheric Christ. This revelation of the etheric Christ will bring us highest insights and powers, if we go to meet this revelation consciously.

Now, when we read in John's Revelation the description of the period of the sixth trumpet, it is remarkable that we find a compelling indication of the importance of this age of the seventh trumpet, hence, the time after the turn of the century. In Revelation, the epoch of the sixth trumpet begins after the following words: "The first woe has passed; behold, two woes are still to come."[184] The description of this epoch ends with the passage: "The second woe has passed; behold the third woe is soon to come." In the 10th chapter of Revelation, still during the time of the sixth trumpet, during the second woe, mention is made of "another mighty angel" whose "face was like the sun." This is the Archangel Michael. In his hand he holds an open book, no longer a sealed one, that contains the world-wisdom. During the time of the sixth trumpet, from 1841 to the year 2000, this wisdom is supposed to be proclaimed to human beings. Michael wishes to transmit yet another special message to human beings, one they must absolutely know about. The way this message is introduced demonstrates its significance:

> And the Angel whom I saw standing on sea and land lifted up his right hand to heaven and swore in the name of Him who bears the life of the world through all the eons, who created heaven and all the creatures in it, earth and all the creatures on it, and the sea and all the creatures in it.[185]

Then follows the message:

> There is no more time! In the days of the trumpet call to be sounded by the seventh Angel, the mystery of God, as He announced to his servants the prophets, will be fulfilled.

And concerning the description of the seventh trumpet it says:

> Then God's temple in heaven was opened, and the altar of the covenant became visible within the temple sanctuary. And there were flashes of lightning, voices sounded, thunder rolled, the earth quaked, and heavy hail filled the air.[186]

If this imaginative-pictorial language is translated into our language and what has been said here about it is taken into consideration, it means that in the age of the seventh trumpet, based on the then developed new faculties, the portal to the spiritual world will be opened wide for those who then live on earth. They will *see* the mystery of that world. It will be a time that can hardly be pictured any worse than it will be, a time of lightning and thunder, of earthquakes and

182

dire weather-related calamities. Voices will become audible, not from humans, but from a higher world. It will be made manifest how human beings and gods are linked together in a mighty task.

Still another connection exists between the time of the seventh trumpet and the present. The seventh trumpet played an important role for Paul and subsequently in Christianity. Paul relates the seventh trumpet to a big epoch that ushers in the end of time and space: "We shall all be changed, suddenly, at the time of the seventh trumpet."[187] At the threshold where time passes on into eternity, the Last Judgment takes place, the separation of human beings into those who tread the path of Christ and those who will tread the path of Ahriman.

Large and small epochs of time, threshold crossings, that stand under the same sign, are related to one another. Thus, these two epochs of time, namely of the seventh trumpet, the large and smaller one, likewise reveal the same, of course to differing degrees. Both epochs denote threshold crossings. What takes place during the mighty crossing of the threshold, when external heaven and earth come to an end and everything returns to the spiritual dimension, likewise takes place in a preparatory sense in the small epoch. New clairvoyant faculties awaken in natural and esoteric developments in people, enabling them to live in the spirit. Even Ahriman begins to make human beings clairvoyant. Through the inner spiritual development, thinking becomes independent of the physical body, the brain, so that it can be taken along into the spirit-world. Ahriman also causes thinking to become independent of the body. The inauguration of a cosmic consciousness, which human beings increasingly have to enliven in themselves, requires a bearer that was prepared through the Mystery of Golgotha by the Christ, namely, the phantom, the resurrection body. Ahriman, too, prepares an etheric body that is supposed to bestow Ahrimanic immortality on human beings. The hour of the "Last Judgment," the hour that will bring about the separation of humanity, already begins in the small epoch of the seventh trumpet and will conclude in the large epoch of the seventh trumpet. A token of it may be that, at the turn of this century, a small and a large epoch, namely the end of a century and of a millennium, coincide. Something of the awesomely dramatic, cosmic earnestness of the last trumpet also infuses and fills the smaller, yet most decisive epoch in regard to humanity's evolution. In it already begins the resounding of the last trumpet. Here, the decision is made, the rest is implementation. According to Rudolf Steiner's statement, now everything depends decisively on human beings. Even helpful intervention by the spirit-world depends on proper human activity.

If we consider what can still be done in the short span of time remaining before the end of the century, two things above all are important: One is the attempt to acquire the most objective view possible of how the outer world may appear at that time. This attempt should be made not only based on thinking but by observing the tendencies that can clearly be perceived today. Secondly, we should realize what kind of efforts the spiritual world had to make in order for all these events to occur on earth in a proper way.

Now, we do not know exactly how the world will appear at the end of the century, but a number of things that have developed and will continue to expand are clearly evident now. We have to understand that spirit-beings are involved in the background of all economic, political, and cultural life. If we do not take these beings seriously, we remain caught up in the darkness of events. On the one side, for example, the retarded Ahrimanic Angels have tremendous power today. They work without any regard for human freedom. Thus, important events in the outer world do not occur at all because of human beings but through these angelic beings. On the other side, Michaelic spirit-beings are active who fully consider human freedom. This is the spiritual reality behind the events that we perceive around us.

In everything that has developed in recent years regarding the growing crime rate and brutality (kidnapping, explosions of bombs, the murder of innocent adults and children, terrorism, anarchism), we have to recognize not only the activity of earthly human beings but that of the dead who rose into the spirit-world with materialistic thoughts. By the end of the century, this will assume the forms of a war of all against all. And everywhere, the "specter of the Roman Empire" lurks as well. It is a danger today among almost all nations. Nearly every country tries to become powerful, more powerful than the others. A few even want to be the most powerful in the world. In the inner direction, such a re-arising "Roman Empire" will turn all people into obedient tools of the leadership. In order to attain this goal, such an "empire" will make use of the strongest means of coercion. In the outward direction, it must produce fear and terror through the stockpiling and brutal power of the most terrible means of destruction. Such a nation has to develop the will to turn itself into the absolute ruling nation on earth.

We have to see more than merely external events in all that America has gone through in recent times and will still go through, such as defeat in Asia and withdrawal from that area, lack of confidence in the government, inflation, and recession. These events are meant to serve America's awakening. In the outer economic and political spheres, the United States will attain the leading position. As long as this happens based on truly genuine democratic volition, a restraining power will issue from it. Free development then remains possible in the spiritual, cultural, and religious spheres. But if the tendencies of the "Roman specter" begin to stir in more and more people, this will lead to a most dangerous development for humanity. That is why the essential battle is for the spiritual awakening in the West.

Let us look back on the events that took place beginning with the onset of the Michael-age until approximately Rudolf Steiner's death (1925). When we call to mind all that led to the realization of spiritual science on earth, so that a large number of people could make it their own, we become aware that mighty preparations continuing through many centuries had to be carried out. Michael fundamentally had to change his pre-Christian activity after the Mystery of Golgotha in order to be able to begin his time-reign in a new sense in 1879. Through supersensible instruction, he had to prepare those connected with him. Christ had to suffer his Passion among humanity which enabled Him, as a consequence of the second Golgotha-Event, to experience the resurrection of His consciousness in human beings who awoke. Through this, the event of Christ's etheric appearance had to be prepared and the new faculties of beholding Him had to mature in the souls. The initiate had to incarnate on earth at the right time, so as to be able to create the new spiritual science; and human beings who could receive it had to be incarnated on earth. If we ponder this comprehensive activity, we become aware of the wise guidance working and creating in all that happens. And we become conscious of the spirit-power, capable of bringing it all about, even in earthly events. We stand in the midst of these spirit-happenings. A part of this mighty process has already become reality, another part is beginning to become earth-reality. But the extent to which the spiritual realities, which still weave above humanity, can become reality on earth also depends on those who can recognize this process, and on how strongly they will engage in it. We are experiencing the dawn of a new spiritual consciousness, of a new age.

AMERICA'S PATH INTO THE FUTURE

America stands at a crossroad. It can continue the materialistic world orientation with all its consequences in the political, economic, and cultural life. Through the degenerate, destructive forces in the social order at the end of the century, America will be forced to face very serious considerations. Through the powerful predicaments this country has suffered in recent years, predicaments that are not yet over, it can also be led to a stronger inner awakening. We can clearly see that the next few years are moving toward a decision. Following World War I, Rudolf Steiner spoke in December of 1919 of the responsibility that the victorious nations have assumed for the civilization of humankind after Germany was ruled out.

> Responsibility will increase that much more for the other side. They will have the actual responsibility. Outward rule will be relatively easily attained. It will be achieved through forces that are not deserved. Like a final necessity of nature, this external transfer of power will occur. But the responsibility will have profound significance for souls. The question has already been inscribed in humanity's book of destiny: Among those to whom will fall external power like an outer necessity, can a sufficient number of people be found, who will sense that they are responsible for the impulses of a spiritual life that will be placed into this purely outward oriented, materialistic rule? For it will be a purely external, materialistic ruling power, do not be fooled about this, a purely superficial, materialistic reign, a culmination of materialistic rule, into which the motivations for a spiritual life will be placed. And this must not come about too slowly.[188]

This was said more than 70 years ago. After World War II, it became evident once again through the victory of the Western Allies that world responsibility for the evolution of civilization among humanity had moved to the West. Rudolf Steiner emphasized in these lectures that this did not refer to individual responsibility but to national responsibility. But it becomes clear that among those nations that now have to bear responsibility, a sufficient number of persons must be found who accept this responsibility, because they can see what it is all about. And the issue is to implant the spiritual seedlings and impulses into the materialistic culture of the West. In so doing, the *spiritual* side of America must be recognized, for it is the soil for these seedlings. We are dealing with the path of Nathaniel, who became a *proper* Israelite and could thus discover the Christ, the Spirit of humanity. And this, likewise, is what it is about in the West.

In this connection it is most interesting that Rudolf Steiner points to a sort of hidden Anthroposophy in America which lives there in a natural way. But this natural predisposition becomes wooden through materialism:

> We in Europe develop Anthroposophy out of the spirit. Over in America, they develop something that is like a kind of wooden doll of Anthroposophy. Everything turns materialistic. But for one who is not a fanatic, American culture has something that resembles what anthroposophical science is in Europe. The only thing is that everything is wooden there. It is not yet alive. We can make it come alive in Europe out of the spirit. People over there take it up instinctively.[189]

This means, it lives in the unconscious, instinctive will of people, but in the materialistic world, cannot fight its way upward into the light. It remains wooden within. Yet, it can assume life through the spirit's activities. Then the rigidified element in human souls melts, as it were, and comes alive. It escapes the sphere of the instincts, racial elements, and blood ties.

It can be comforting to realize that a kind of hidden impulse of a spiritual Christianity is effective in the West, for that is Anthroposophy. When we carry the light of spiritual insight down into the night of the will, that realm does become lighter. The so-called "wooden man" can be liberated and come alive:

> The time will come eventually when this American "wooden man"—and everybody is in fact such a "wooden being" at this point—will begin to speak. Then it will have to say something similar to this to European Anthroposophy.[190]

When will this hidden form of Anthroposophy begin to speak? Already in the present—whenever people allow spiritual thoughts into their minds and digest them!

Through today's intellectual thoughts, the "wooden man" turns into stone, like the giant in Goethe's "Fairy Tale" who turned immobile in front of the Temple of Humanity. He awakens to life through thoughts that in themselves are alive. In the future, the enlivening of the inner human being is moving toward a culmination. In the same lecture by Rudolf Steiner, we read something quite astounding, especially if we call to mind that the actual manifestation of the American Cultural Epoch will be fulfilled in the seventh Post-Atlantean Age.

> As I have told you, the vernal equinox is now in Pisces. Earlier, it was in Aries. In the time to come it will be in the sign of Aquarius. It is then that the

proper American civilization will arise. Until then, more and more elements of civilization will move across to America. One who is willing to see this can notice even now how powerful Americans are becoming, while Europe is slowly becoming more and more ineffective. . . . Civilization is shifting over to America. It is a slow process. But when the sun with its vernal equinox will enter the sign of Aquarius, its rays will shine down so favorably upon the earth that American culture and civilization will become especially powerful.[191]

Regarding Europe, this asserts that the old conditions of civilization will die down there and that Europe can only live based on new spiritual impulses which are indeed growing strongly there. If a zenith of American evolution can be attained as early as the sixth Post-Atlantean Period of the earth, will it be a spiritual culmination?

This is what is so interesting. In America, materialism is truly rampant and yet is on the way to the spirit. When a European becomes a materialist, his or her human element dies. Americans are young materialists. Actually, all children are materialists and then grow up to what is not materialism. And so, crude American materialism will develop directly into something spiritual. And this will come to pass when the sun stands in the sign of Aquarius.[192]

Rudolf Steiner then said that it was based on the above insights that the task could be recognized that one has toward the spiritual side in regard to America. For we have to sow the seeds for the spiritualization of the coming culture already today. We can only do that properly by taking America's own spiritual forces into consideration, forces that are latent in the

West. This way, we forge the spirit-sword with which to take up the battle against the Ahrimanic falsification of the Western attitude of soul through the Ahrimanic powers. Along with Ahriman's incarnation, these powers wish to give the whole civilization in the Western world their own direction. Through an ever more powerful materialism, this civilization is supposed to harden human thinking, feeling, and will so that the human etheric body will solidify to such an extent that it cannot dissolve after death. The dead would thus remain cut off from the spiritual world and would be compelled to establish an Ahrimanic earth. Then, no possibility would exist for them to develop a human, immortal ego. As ego-less group souls, they would be forced to serve Ahriman.

One can understand why the Angels, who are in the service of Michael and are active among human beings, try to instill in them the impulse not to feel happy or content on earth as long as others are unhappy. If we consider the terrible fate of those who succumb today to materialism, then this painful experience can give rise to the most powerful impulse to become so strong in our own inner development that forces of help and salvation can flow down from higher beings into us, so that we can wrest such humans away from Ahriman. It will be a battle for each and every human soul until the end of earth evolution. But this way Anthroposophy will turn into something quite different. Aside from the thorough study of its thoughts, people will resort much more to Rudolf Steiner's book, *Knowledge of the Higher Worlds and Its Attainment*. Universal healing forces, forces that redeem human beings, can mature in the human soul, even if they develop slowly, when, aside from the necessary work [through study] of acquiring knowledge, we focus equally and even more strongly on the unfolding of our inner capacities. This is not said in order to express moral sentiments. It is said because, when we try to look at America from a spiritual standpoint, the following insight impresses itself on our mind: Here, more powerful forces have to be called into play, if one wishes not only to bear up to the opposing powers but to push them back into their justified bounds. The Ahrimanic environment demands more of human beings. People have to change in such a world; that becomes obvious. The following sentences from the book, *Knowledge of the Higher Worlds and Its Attainment* assume more weight:

> Those who seek for the secrets of human nature through perception of their own must follow the golden rule of true spiritual science. And this *golden* rule is: When you try to take *one* step forward in the perception of esoteric truths, simultaneously take *three* steps forward in perfecting your character toward the good.[193]

Also, when we read in "Inner Realities of Evolution" about the concept of creative renunciation and resignation and how we can thereby develop forces that are particularly effective spiritually, this can assume special importance.[194] Particularly in America, significant possibilities for developing these forces exist. Part of this is to become painstakingly familiar with and to make a detailed actual study of Ahriman's activity and all its ramifications. If this were not done, we would be severely negligent. The battle that must be waged here was inscribed already 2000 years ago into America's history through the deed of the one who came from the Sun and, as a Sun-initiate and in full accord with the Golgotha-Event, overthrew the Ahrimanic black magician. He could vanquish him by means of the Christ-forces that shone forth anew in earth's evolution.

This spirit battle can be waged today in such a way that one's own inner capabilities thereby steadily grow stronger. As was indicated, Melville had an inkling of this. In the white whale, who for Ahab was purely a symbol of all evil, devilish powers on earth, Ishmael could see the sign of death and resurrection and the path pursued by Jonah, who, swallowed up by the whale, was returned to life after three days. Jonah became familiar with the whale from within through his experience of death and resurrection. It gives one quite a different point of view in regard to evil in the world, especially in regard to Ahriman, a free sovereign attitude. This comes to expression in a significant remark by Rudolf Steiner:

> People must learn to interpret life based on spiritual science in order to recognize and learn to master the trends that lead toward Ahriman's incarnation. They will have to know that Ahriman will live among them on earth and that they will confront him, deciding on their own what they wish to learn and accept from him. But they will not be able to do that if they do not take in hand certain spiritual or even unspiritual movements, which Ahriman otherwise will use in order to leave human beings as much as possible in the dark concerning his coming. . . .[195]

Lauenstein states that the battle with the whale represents a voluntary encounter with death.[196]

In the West, it is a matter of a conscious encounter with Ahriman's death-forces, an encounter carried out in freedom. We have to have the courage to come to know the dragon, the whale, death, or Ahriman from within, otherwise we cannot prevail against him at all. In the spiritual battle with the death-forces, the human being can bring his ego to birth as a new force. In the lecture, "Human Evolution, World Soul, and

Cosmic Spirit," Rudolf Steiner describes the ego as a warrior against death. He describes how a constant death-process takes place in the human being, a process that slowly undermines life:

> If you grasp how the ego is a constant fighter against this process of death, then you have understood that the ego is something which, as such, has nothing to do with death; you have graphically understood something that otherwise is designated dialectically or logically as immortality.[197]

The ego is the constant warrior against death. It comes to birth in us in the struggle against death. Thus we attain our immortality. We must not recoil from seeing death or taking up the fight against death, against Ahriman. In the last commentary to his *Leading Thoughts*, Rudolf Steiner concludes with the words:

> In a science of the spirit, the other sphere is now created in which an Ahrimanic element is not present at all. And it is through knowledge-filled acceptance of that spirituality, to which the Ahrimanic powers have *no* access, that we are strengthened to confront Ahriman *in the world*.[198]

The battle against Ahriman's forces must be waged in full accord with the Christ-impulse as inaugurated by Him *today,* 2000 years after Golgotha. We must look at the second Golgotha-Event and the present activity of the etheric Christ. From Him, we can attain the death-vanquishing resurrection forces for our time. This is the most important event occurring in our age: "It is the greatest secret of our age: the secret of the Second Coming of Christ. . . ."[199] It is the all-surpassing, most luminous event of our century, the greatest event since the Mystery of Golgotha. The appearance of Christ in the etheric world must be viewed as the spiritual center through which *all* spiritual activity on earth is inspired and illuminated. Considering that Anthroposophy itself is a gift of the etherically appearing Christ, who suffered death of consciousness in the etheric world in order to resurrect in the human consciousness soul, we clearly recognize the profound importance of this event. Then we can understand why Rudolf Steiner said with greatest emphasis and earnestness:

> And all anthroposophical teachings should be transformed in us into the overriding wish not to allow this event to bypass humanity without a trace. . . .[200]

Or:

> Spiritual science prepares human beings for this event; prepares them to fit in the proper way into the age and to see, with bright reasoning and clarity of insight, what is truly present yet could pass them by, without their being able to make it fruitful for themselves: This is what it is all about.[201]

When we call to mind how the Ahrimanic opposing forces do all in their power to cause this event to pass us by, and how they work to put another being in place of the Christ, then we see another side of the confrontation with Ahriman in the West. If the struggle against Ahriman's destructive forces is eventually taken up here *consciously*, because it is demanded by this continent, it will have significance for the rest of the world and for the events that are impending now. Rudolf Steiner was often pained by the fact that the members did not take his words realistically enough. This becomes evident in the following remarks:

> The opponents have taken up their positions. The opponents are intensifying the battle. Our struggle and capabilities are weak, quite weak. And our perception of Anthroposophy is in many respects a sleepy, quite a sleepy one. This is the great pain that today burdens the shoulders of one who fully sees through these things.[202]

Another form of non-comprehension of the Christ-being comes from the East. A guru can arrive from India and speak in the West of Christianity's significance. He can speak of the profound truth hidden in the words, "The kingdom of heaven is in you," or, "Christ in us," He can speak of the truth of the words, "I am the light of the world." More profoundly than clergymen can say it today, he can speak of words such as, "Unless one is born anew, he cannot ascend to the kingdom of God."[203] Such a guru may even be able to distinguish between Jesus and Christ and yet might not see the essence of the Christ-Event on earth. He would say that Christ Jesus was a son of God, as is every guru; that the "guru-power" or "God's power" or even the "Christ-power" is present in every master; that it is not something that is merely human, but something divine. And yet, in this way one cannot understand the essence of the Christ-Event, nor even the significance of the spiritual-etheric reappearance of the Christ in our time. For, why should Christ reappear, when He said: "I am with you all the days until the end of the world?" A higher being than could previously be reached appeared in the Christ. With His Coming, a turning point of time occurred. The old earth began to disappear and a new earth and humanity began to develop from out of forces that, until then, had not been connected to the earth. This cannot be understood, unless the East is guided to the most important event of our age, the appearance of the etheric Christ. The events around the turn of the century are illuminated by the working of the etheric Christ and the one who is the countenance of Christ in our time: Michael. Christ is the spiritual leader in all these events. One can experience how a certain mood of expectation is present in America among many religious and spiritually seeking people for the "Second Coming of Christ." This mood of expectation can direct one toward the right or false goals. A right mood of expectation is the greatest help for what is to come:

> The spirit of our age should be the spirit of expectation. It should be the spirit that, out of such expectation, should develop a comprehension for the great experience, born out of the suffering of the first half of the 20th century. But if in truth we do not look upon all that is a hindrance for us, we will not be able to meet this event today.[204]

The event of Christ's Second Coming, which begins at the present, will take hold of more and more people in the next 3000 years, according to Rudolf Steiner. It will lead them to behold Christ and will become more and more strongly effective on earth. It will accompany us until the time of the sixth cultural epoch, the epoch that is under the sign of Aquarius. That is the epoch of an American spiritual culture. At the same time, the unfolding of the spirit-self in the East of Europe will occur. Whether it can come to this in the West depends on the events around the turn of this century. It depends on whether the good spiritual stream will be successful in attaining a spiritual breakthrough in the world and whether spiritual seedlings can be successfully implanted in

America in the materialistic civilization. Rudolf Steiner raised the question, as was mentionned earlier:

> Will . . . a sufficiently large number of people be found who feel the responsibility of . . . placing the impulses for a spiritual life into the culmination of the materialistic rule?[205]

When we look at the handful of people who take a stand for a new spiritual science in America today, we might question whether that is "a sufficient number of people," considering the vast territory of America and the minuscule number of people who identify with and stand up for the spirit here. These few are indeed extraordinarily active in the various areas of science, in sociology, bio-dynamic agriculture, the Waldorf school movement, artistic activities, and the Movement for Religious Renewal. The anthroposophical work in branches and groups is, of course, especially important. Here, one always carries this question by Rudolf Steiner in one's heart: "Will . . . a sufficiently large number of people be found," who are willing to assume responsibility for what can come into being particularly here, people who can see the spiritual predispositions of the West, predispositions in which rest the contribution that the West can make for the whole of humanity? When we observe the activities of the counter-forces, it is a difficult but also a most significant task.

Rudolf Steiner was of the conviction that this task can be carried out, if the other, deeper America and the true Europe can be found:

> The true American spirit is the very element that will eventually unite with the spirit of Europe, which has to discover its task in a more spiritual way. And if something like this is studied in this way, we see how we basically have to conduct ourselves in the world.[206]

Part III: Ralph Waldo Emerson – A Herald of the Future

Reflections on Emerson, Goethe, and Rudolf Steiner

The "Human" Aspect in the Human Being

In Emerson lived a strong desire to know what the human being is in his innermost essence. This was the question that lived in him, not the question of belonging to a nationality or race.

Out of his spiritual, transcendental world view, Emerson recognized that the divine creative spirit permeates the whole universe, the kingdoms of nature, and all human beings. He felt that it was the main task for every person to become conscious of this fact. He was convinced that awareness of the creative spirit in world and nature would make an inner resurrection possible for human beings. They would thus discover a deeper meaning for their life on earth; they would discover the "human being" within themselves. Through this discovery, they would be able to begin, by way of a new perception, to unite with the cosmic spirit. In this way, people themselves would acquire the possibility of becoming creative spirits and, with that, turn into free, independent beings. This is also the deepest motive of Anthroposophy in the 20th century. Anthroposophy can penetrate even further into the secrets of the human being and his connection to the higher world than could Emerson in the 19th century. Emerson knew of this future development. A "hidden Anthroposophy" lived in

Emerson initially as an "instinct" which, then, became ever clearer and more conscious. He spoke of three stages. During the first stage, we discover that spiritual "instincts" live in our soul. During the second, we begin to form an opinion of these instincts; still, opinions are subjective. We have to reach a third stage and attain a spiritual knowledge that no longer is subjective.

With this desire to develop higher stages of knowledge and consciousness (instinct—opinion—knowledge), Emerson reveals himself as a man of the age of the consciousness soul. This makes evident his inner relationship to what Anthroposophy later on had to bring.

EMERSON'S RELATIONSHIP TO GOETHE

Ralph Waldo Emerson was born on May 25, 1803 in Boston. He became a minister there in 1826. For health reasons he had to interrupt his activity. Later, in 1829, he became a minister of the Second Unitarian Congregation. He married, but his wife died 18 months later. He left the church in 1832. He embarked on a new life, for his inner wealth was greater than what the churches with their frequently dogmatic views could allow. He became an independent writer, a renowned philosopher, and a well known poet. It was an inner breakthrough to newly awakening forces, a breakthrough to his true being. In the biography of every person, the 28th year is most important, for the forces of youth begin to wane. Something new must be developed, otherwise the young person soon experiences an emptiness and impotence in his soul. This can easily cause him to break with all earlier ideas and ideals. It is a dramatic experience of thousands of young people who then end up in the ranks of the hopeless, passive, materialistic masses or turn into radical revolutionaries.

For Emerson, this was the most important point of his life. When his 29th year approached, he felt growing emptiness and discontent in his soul. But in contrast to the masses or the revolutionaries, he kindled a new fire in the depths of his soul. He first felt his awakening deeper faculties, his "spiritual instincts," in an instinctive, dreamy way, and they forced him to transform his whole life. He had the courage to do it. He became conscious of his inner potential, a true calling, and in this way developed into an extraordinary personality.

After Emerson had left the church, he felt a powerful longing to become acquainted with people who were spiritually related to him. In Europe, he could encounter such people. Among them was Carlyle in England, a faithful admirer of Johann Wolfgang von Goethe, who had passed away in the year 1832, the year when Emerson's whole life changed. Encouraged by Carlyle, Emerson began with the study of Goethe, something he continued for many years in a most thorough manner. We can find out much about his inner kinship with Goethe from his book, *Representative Men*, in which he writes about Plato, Swedenborg, Montaigne, Shakespeare, Napoleon, and Goethe. In the chapter, "Goethe, the Writer," Emerson indicates that he viewed Goethe as representative of all writers. Emerson not only valued Goethe's poetic works, but also his differing views and revolutionary endeavors in the scientific field. Emerson studied Goethe's theory of color, a theory which proves that colors (by contrast to Newton's view) appear in the interplay of light and darkness. In addition, he studied the archetypal plant (Urpflanze). In *Representative Men*, he writes:

> He (Goethe) has contributed a key to many parts
> of nature through the rare turn for unity and simplic-
> ity in his mind. Thus Goethe suggested the leading

idea of modern botany, that a leaf or the eye of a leaf is the unit of botany, and that every part of a plant is only a transformed leaf to meet a new condition; and by varying the conditions, a leaf may be converted into any other organ, and any other organ into a leaf.

Concerning Goethe's theory of color, he wrote:

In optics again he rejected the artificial theory of seven colors, and considered that every color was the mixture of light and darkness in new proportions.[1]

The ray of light passes invisible through space and only when it falls on an object is it seen.[2]

Emerson's thoughts about Goethe's scientific research show how closely related he felt to Goethe and how much he occupied himself with the results of Goethe's research. Of course, he never met Goethe; his brother did.

RUDOLF STEINER ON EMERSON'S COMPREHENSION OF GOETHE

When Emerson died in 1882, Rudolf Steiner was 21 years old. He was a student at the Technical College (Technische Hochschule) in Vienna, where he heard lectures by Karl Julius Schröer and became acquainted with him. Through Schröer, Rudolf Steiner became thoroughly and intimately familiar with Goethe's works, since Schröer, a professor of German literature, was a renowned expert on Goethe.

From this time on, Goethe became a guiding star for Rudolf Steiner. At age 21, Rudolf Steiner received an invitation to publish Goethe's scientific works in Kürschner's "German National Literature."[3] Through Rudolf Steiner's introductions to this work, Goethe's scientific discoveries appeared in their true light and actual significance. Four years later, in 1886, Rudolf Steiner published his book, *Grundlinien einer Erkenntnistheorie der Goetheschen Weltanschauun.*[4] In 1890, Steiner moved to Weimar where he became an associate in the Goethe and Schiller Archive. Through his books and lectures, Rudolf Steiner introduced many people to Goethe in a new way. He led them to a deeper, more inward understanding of Goethe's discoveries and poetic works.

In *Menschenschicksale und Völkerschicksale (The Destinies of Individuals and of Nations)* , Steiner spoke about two chapters in Emerson's *Representative Men,* those about Shakespeare and Goethe. But before he started with this, he revealed something quite unique about Emerson.

In every human being, said Rudolf Steiner, lives a dreamer, and in some people this dreamer has a powerful connection to the spiritual world. Without their being aware of it, this dreamer influences their thinking, feeling, and will. They frequently act out of a more profound wisdom. In most people, this activity remains completely in the unconscious. But Emerson had a certain conscious perception of this inner guidance. He spoke, for example, of the "spiritual instincts" of human beings, which they gradually ought to permeate with consciousness. Rudolf Steiner said that a personality as significant as Emerson was inspired by his guiding angel; and this angel, in turn, had a connection to the higher beings of the spiritual hierarchies. In this way, Emerson was often inspired.

We carry a dreamer within us. We all carry within us a subtle human being. When we function as we do on earth, with our thoughts, feelings, and will, that

205

is what Earth-evolution has given us. But something has remained in us of the Moon-evolution: a dreaming human being. In this dreamer, more is given to us than what we can have in our thoughts, feelings and will impulses.[5]

And he added the following words:

> The inspirations of the Angels play into our dreams. They, in turn, are inspired by beings of the higher hierarchies.[6]

Rudolf Steiner indicated that the dreamer in Emerson made it possible for him to look more deeply into individuals like Shakespeare and Goethe. He could penetrate their inner soul nature more thoroughly. By giving a few examples of how Emerson evaluated Shakespeare and Goethe, Rudolf Steiner demonstrated that, through the dreamer in his soul's depths, Emerson could make more profound statements about the various attitudes of soul among English and Central Europeans.

Rudolf Steiner characterized the English as human beings who live in the consciousness soul. They view the outer world as observers. They look consciously and clearly at events that take place around them, even at the historical developments. Emerson described Shakespeare as a poet who receives his themes not so much from his inner being but from outside; he is stimulated by events in history. With the aid of his artistic abilities, he can turn these stimuli into splendid drama:

> Shakespeare knew that tradition supplies a better fable than any invention can. Even if he lost any credit of design, he augmented his resources; and, at that day, our petulant demand for originality was not so

much pressed. There was no literature for the millions. The universal reading, the cheap press, were unknown. A great poet who appears in illiterate times, absorbs into his sphere all the light which is anywhere radiating. Every intellectual jewel, every flower of sentiment, it is his fine office to bring these to his people; and he comes to value his memory equally with his invention. He is therefore little solicitous whence his thoughts have been derived; whether through translation, whether through tradition, whether by travel in distant countries, whether by inspiration; from whatever source, they are equally welcome to his uncritical audience.[7]

When Emerson spoke of Goethe, he spoke with inner understanding and sympathy, because he felt akin to him:

What is strange too, he lived in a small town, in a petty state, in a defeated state, and in a time when Germany played no leading part in the world's affairs as to swell the bosom of her sons with any metropolitan pride, such as might have cheered a French or English, or once, a Roman or Attic genius. Yet there is no trace of provincial limitation in his muse. He is not a debtor to his position, but was born with a free and controlling genius.[8]

Emerson's opinion of Goethe was that it was not his environment that formed him and his writings, but only what he had within him, what he had brought with him, his "free and controlling genius," his ego. What Emerson saw in Goethe, has to do with the soul mentality of the German people. Different nations have different missions. England's task was to develop the consciousness soul; Germany's mission was to develop the ego, the "I", the human being's true center. Shakespeare was inspired more by the surrounding environment and its historic events, while Goethe was inspired more out of the innermost center of his being. Thus, Emerson had recognized something of two very different soul dispositions in two nations and the differing missions resulting from them.

In the lectures mentioned earlier, Rudolf Steiner spoke about the way in which Emerson described Goethe:

> And now we turn to Emerson's affectionate characterization of Goethe. He described Goethe as the one who is representative of a writer. And Emerson says about Goethe: Nature everywhere depends on someone revealing her wondrous works. Every stone, plant, and every creature in nature wait for the time when they will be expressed by the soul of the human being. The writer will always have an intimate connection with nature. It is as if the Creator Himself had prepared the thought that in time the writer should come into being. It is strange, so says Emerson in reference to Goethe, how in regard to his gift, this man owed nothing to his nation, his country, or his environment, but how everything poured forth out of himself. Even over truth and error, Goethe alone decided; everything originated out of himself. Or he said of Goethe: "In my eyes, the writer exemplifies a man whose position was predestined during the forming of the world."

And Rudolf Steiner added to this:

> Emerson characterized Shakespeare as one who behaves the way the general public expects; Goethe as a man who had been ordained from the beginning of the world; who owed nothing to the profession or position he occupied. He entered this world at birth as a free, vigilant genius. . . .[9]

EMERSON,
HELPER OF AMERICA'S FUTURE

THE SPIRITUAL FORCE IN EMERSON

As was described earlier, Rudolf Steiner speaks of the threat of the double, a being within the human being, possessed of cold intelligence and instinctively effective, primitively elemental will. These beings live in every human being. If their effects are too powerful, ego-less humans would be the result, people open to any ambition by spirit-alienated leaders. This is the ideal of certain secret groups in America. Their members believe that, through an America thus prepared and synchronized, they can assume the leadership-role over humanity. This would work against Europe's efforts toward a new, higher, spiritual-scientific knowledge that leads to inner individual development for each person. Rudolf Steiner states concerning Emerson's spiritual view, which to a large part was inspired by European cultural life, especially by Goethe, that it protected him from falling prey to the double's forces. He then refers to two different streams in America:

> It is true that two opposites are developing. Under the influences described today, individuals like Emerson evolve, who place their fully developed human qualities over against the double. On the other side, there are those who develop like Woodrow Wilson, individuals who are merely an encasing for the double, through whom the double works particularly powerfully. Such people are essentially embodiments of American geographic nature.[10]

Using these two personalities as examples, Rudolf Steiner here characterizes two different possible developments in America. Furthermore, this shows how important Emerson is for an understanding of America, if one wishes to support the spiritual direction here. It is of great significance that an impulse was effective in Emerson that can set limitations for the double's forces by means of a spiritual viewpoint of the world and of the human being. It is easy to become depressed in America, when, without such a spiritual world view, one observes the almost unlimited activity of these negative forces, or when one experiences how difficult it is for people to assess the weight of such facts correctly. Then the joy is that much greater when a true inner breakthrough occurs in individuals, and they begin to transform outer life through the spirit. If Emerson's impulse would be taken up in America and developed further in accordance with the 20th century, as Anthroposophy tries to do, something significant, yes, even decisive could originate from that. We must not underestimate the impulse that a personality like Ralph Waldo Emerson brought to life in America, for that impulse was born here.

Rudolf Steiner stated that earnest spiritual work produces a force that, although it cannot eliminate the Ahrimanic effects, can curtail them to the extent that, through both forces working together, the good and the opposing force, something beneficial results for humanity's development. Moreover, we must not forget that Emerson's spirit grew out of the combined effects of what America developed in him and what he absorbed from the European spirit. Such spiritual cooperation between America and Europe must be increasingly realized, for much depends on it for humanity.

EMERSON, THINKER OF A SPIRITUAL VIEW

Why is it so important to speak of Ralph Waldo Emerson in America when seeking a modern path of inner development? What can Emerson, who died a century ago, signify for our age?

Brooks Atkinson writes of Emerson: "Gentle, kindly, and upright, he was the teacher of America."[11] When we can attain deeper insight into Emerson and his writings, and when we gradually find a path to the temple concealed within his innermost being, a temple in which the divine was present, then we will find something that can convince us that Emerson was not only the right spiritual teacher for the America of his time, but for today as well. Emerson predicted that new faculties would awaken in human consciousness, that would be able to develop out of the Western soul mentality, faculties that would make it possible to research the diversity of the spiritual world. These faculties are most important for the future of humankind.

It is equally important that Emerson could unite Europe and America in his soul. Stephen E. Whicher writes in his biography of Emerson: "There is a secret fount of power in him, a fire within 'under the Andes.' That is felt in all his works without being identifiable in any."[12]

Whicher continues that we have not been fully able to discover this "secret fount" of spiritual power in Emerson, this core of his nature, from which the fire of his spirit flamed forth. This fountainhead of the spirit springs from a Western state of soul. Emerson demanded that America should not just passively imitate what emerged from Europe; she should discover her own being, and, out of it, make her contribution to the development of humanity. Emerson was familiar with the European world view and was influenced by it, but he worked based on a spiritual source of his own and his Western mentality.

We should ponder Emerson's most outstanding ideas for some time, if we want to comprehend their importance for humanity as well as for individual development. His thoughts are not only capable of giving America's evolution a new direction, but they can also illuminate the special contribution the West has to make toward the progress of humankind.

Emerson was convinced that the intellect can only grasp the laws and forces at work in the physical world, not the spiritual forces that create and shape this world. He spoke of two different forms of thinking: the first is the "mathematical, logical" thinking of today; the second he called "intuitive thinking." With the latter, it is possible to discover the workings of spiritual forces in the world of perceptions. Intuitive, will-like thinking is an active thinking that belongs to deeper human potentials. Such a thinking has to be more strongly developed today in contrast to the first form of "head-thinking," the thinking that is incapable of exploring the creative activity of the Creator Spirit in the universe. Emerson stated that a unique soul dwells in every human being. Like everything on earth, it is penetrated by the creative World Spirit. This World Spirit forms and shapes, enlivens and ensouls the visible world, even the human physical body; it works in each of his organs and limbs.

> All goes to show that the soul in man is not an organ, but animates and exercises all the organs; is not a function, like the power of memory, of calculation, of comparison, but uses these as hands and feet; is not a faculty, but a light; is not the intellect or will, but the master of the intellect and the will; is the background of our being, in which they lie; —an immensity not possessed and that cannot be pos-

sessed. From within or from behind, a light shines through us upon things and makes us aware that we are nothing, but the light is all. A man is the facade of a temple wherein all wisdom and all good abide. What we commonly call man, the eating, drinking, planting, counting man, does not, as we know him, represent himself, but misrepresents himself. Him we do not respect, but the soul, whose organ he is, would he let it appear through his action, would make our knees bend. When it breathes through his intellect, it is genius; when it breathes through his will, it is virtue; when it flows through his affection, it is love.[13]

This higher soul works in all organs of the physical body, in the functions of the forces of life and growth, in all the abilities of its being. It reveals itself in three ways: as intelligence or wisdom in our thinking, as virtue in our will, as love in our heart. Emerson stated that the soul, the higher self, creates the body, not the other way around. First, the soul is present, the body, only afterwards. He does not say that body and soul are two totally different things that have nothing to do with each other, one belonging to the earthly, the other to the divine world and created by it. He says that the higher soul is effective in each physical organ, each function of the body, in all its bodily forces, as well as in its own soul forces— in thinking, feeling, and willing. When we become conscious of the soul's activity in ourselves, we strengthen the soul. And in that way, we slowly learn to master our forces and abilities. This process of mastering ourselves proceeds from the enlivening of our higher soul, which in turn is permeated by God. The body is a marvelous instrument on which our higher soul plays. The body is the temple in which God, the Creator Spirit, works. "And the blindness of the intellect," says Emerson, "begins when it would be something of itself. The weakness of the will begins when the individual would be something of himself."[14]

If the intellect were to say that it alone matters, it would turn blind; if the will would say that activity, deeds alone are all that matters, it would become tyrannical. And if love would suppose that it alone could suffice, it would become egotistic. All three would be wrong. Our higher soul, we could also say, our higher, creative self, works through each of the three forces, through love, knowledge, and will. In this way, the soul is connected with the Creator Spirit of the world. Without this unity, it would be nothing.

Emerson did not speak in philosophical abstractions. He made an effort to live in realities and to penetrate perceptually to spiritual and earthly actualities. When we keep in our minds a lively concept of our higher soul, our higher self, we also learn to experience Emerson's words more deeply: "All reform aims in some one particular to let the soul have its way through us; in other words, to engage us to obey."[15]

This means: Always follow your higher self. In it lives the Creator Spirit of the world. Identify with Him and His spirit-power will stream through you and the world.

When we study Emerson, our attention is drawn to his spiritual relationship with nature. He recognized that the whole of nature came out of the spirit and returns to it again.

> The divine circulations never rest nor linger. Nature is the incarnation of a thought, and turns to a thought again, as ice becomes water and gas. The world is mind precipitated, and the volatile essence is forever escaping again into the state of free thought.[16]

We can recognize how the creative, formative spirit is revealed in all processes of nature. We stand, as it were, on holy ground, we walk through "holy land" when we walk through meadows and forests or climb up hills. God lives and works in nature. We breathe His presence. And since we are a part of nature, we too are a manifestation of His holy presence. We are His image. The idea of God professed by Christianity was too narrow for Emerson. In him lived Paul's thought, who said of God: "He is not far from any one of us, for in Him we live, move, and have our being."[17]

Our senses observe external phenomena; our thinking observes the work of eternal thoughts that reign within these phenomena. We live in a world in which divine thoughts of the primal beginning changed into creative words, and the creative words then became flesh.

A TIME OF TRANSITION

Emerson had the distinct feeling that he lived in a time of important transition. It was a time when the old and traditional became powerless and decadent, but it was also a time in which new ideas and impulses arose and began to determine life. In "The Conduct of Life," he says:

> We live in a transition period, when the old faiths which comforted nations, and not only so but made nations, seem to have spent their force. . . . The lover of the old religion complains that our contemporaries, scholars as well as merchants, succumb to a great despair,—have corrupted into a timorous conservatism and believe in nothing.[18]

He clearly recognized that something new would have to come, indeed, that it was on the way. And he was preparing it.
Emerson lived strongly in his will-sphere, in his spiritual "instincts," and was closely connected with the Creator Spirit

of the world. He tried to be conscious of Him. Through this inner connection, he had become receptive for what was developing in his age. He sensed that something decisive was about to come. Particularly during the years when he was most creatively active, from 1841 until a few years prior to his death in 1882, a powerful change in the spiritual reign of our epoch occurred in the sphere of the spiritual world directly adjacent to our earth. Emerson was intuitively conscious of this fact. He perceived that the ancient sources had lost their power of inspiration and that new ones would have to be opened up. In an essay, he wrote: "Great men have always done so, and confided themselves childlike to the genius of their age. . . . "[19]

Emerson could not behold what was going on in the realm of the "genius of the age," but he could experience it through his inner unity with the Creative Spirit of the world. If one would become aware of this connection to the genius of one's age, one would attach greater weight to Emerson's position in his age. The dreamer in him experienced this link.

Others likewise sensed this. In his book, *Ein Weiser Amerikas spricht zu uns* (A Wise Man from America Speaks to Us), the German author Hans Hartmann gives us an excellent introduction to Emerson's life and his spiritual outlook on the human being and the world:

> We will only do him justice and come closer to him when we free ourselves from the prejudice that "perceptions" about nature, human being, and God can be acquired in a discursive way, meaning, by logically moving from one thought, one sentence, one thesis to the next. Due to his whole conduct of life, his characteristic thinking, his *having to* think, Emerson felt tremendous alienation from all logical, dogmatic thinking. If it is true that we are now passing beyond an epoch of dogmatic thinking—perhaps in context

with the Platonic year—, a thinking often designated by Emerson as fanaticism, into an epoch of more flexible, far more conscious thinking and contemplation, directed more to the essential, to the limits of events, words, and concepts, then Emerson has been one of the greatest forerunners and pioneers of this epoch.[20]

If one does not have the right inner attitude toward Emerson, one does not recognize what constitutes his actual significance. Then, one does not develop an organ of comprehension for him.

EMERSON AND AMERICA

Through his inner connection with the spirit, Emerson could see America differently. Edgar Lee Masters describes it in the following way:

There was a great ruggedness in this tall, thin-chested, spare and ascetic looking philosopher. There was the kind of understanding which sang the American spirit instead of patriotism, which stood for truth rather than regularity.[21]

Emerson saw and experienced something of America's invisible spirit. He regarded the America of his age not merely from outer viewpoints. He had an inner relationship to his country. He never remained within the limitations of narrow nationalism. Instead, he had a concrete, direct sense for what America's task might be in world evolution. He said that Americans should not merely consider the welfare of their own country, they should become world citizens. On the one side, he could find hard words to say about the materialistic, egotistical, self-serving American. Sadly, he recognized that most

Americans had lost their faith in and hope for something greater than mere concerns for everyday life.

On the other side, in his address, "The American Scholar," Emerson said: "A nation of men will for the first time exist, because each believes himself inspired by the Divine Soul which also inspires all men."22 Note the last words: ". . . which . . . inspires *all* men." This does away with all narrow nationalism. Emerson was involved with concerns of humanity.

In the same address, when Emerson drew his listeners' attention to the fact that culturally America was still quite dependent on Europe and that she would yet have to develop her own self-awareness in order to recognize what her own cultural contribution to humanity might be, he did not refer to a nationalistic nation but, based on his own deeper insight, to America's hidden spirituality. He knew that all the imitating of foreign countries would destroy America's inner potential, her hidden realistic idealism, her "spiritual instincts," America has to grasp everything *anew* and make it her own through her own forces.

If America and her people would follow the spirit that inspires all human beings, new forces could unfold—like plants after a refreshing rain—and change the present lifestyle of Americans. This could take place, said Emerson, because a higher form of thinking, a heart open to all humanity, a spiritualized will could develop out of the same inner forces. This would mean that America would also arrive at a spiritual understanding of her own being.

Earlier in this book, a description was given of how Ahriman himself will incarnate in America. This is the dark cloud of destiny that could extinguish all efforts toward recognizing and changing America's spiritual condition. This is an important goal of the opposing forces.

In view of the present condition, it would not be possible to penetrate America completely with a spiritual world view already now, so that Emerson's ideal might become a reality. What does matter is that a growing number of Americans can form a spiritual picture of America with all her future possibilities and great dangers, and that they can then remain mindful of such a spiritually envisioned America and recognize the opposing powers. *That* is the sword that Americans ought to forge—as did Siegfried—in order to overcome the dragon through their spirit-enlightened insight.

They have to know the issues confronting them in the West. And that is what the opposing powers fear and try to prevent by all means. Nothing else could be more dangerous for them. Americans must therefore become capable of setting limits for the opposing powers. Rudolf Steiner explained that out of just such a battle could come what the good powers are aiming for. Creative ideas and strong forces of the will, born through the forging of one's own spirit-sword, could call forth impulses for a renewal of cultural life, a spirit of true democracy, and a recovery of the economic life.

Why is it that so many young people show so much promise but cannot develop their potential? Why do these capacities atrophy in their souls after a time? The bearers of these faculties become tired, lose their faith and, without hope for a better future, give themselves up completely to the life of the moment. This is the reason why they accept the America as we know her today as the only possibility, and deny the America of the future that dwells in their own depths of soul.

Out of his insight that the Creative Spirit with Its power of ideas is a reality in the world, and that It permeates all existence and events and thus can inspire and enthuse man as well for the higher goals revealed in It, Emerson envisioned the possibility of developing the deeper forces inherent in young Americans by way of schools and universities. Based on such visions, he uttered the words: "A nation of men will for the first time exist, because each believes himself inspired by the Divine Soul which inspires all men."

This can only be achieved when a spiritual connection can come about between the representatives of the Central European spirit and those of a spiritually viewed America. This was Rudolf Steiner's conviction. This is why it is of decisive importance that a deeper, helpful understanding for America can grow in Central Europe. It will have to be recognized that, without such help, America will move toward extremely difficult times, and with America, so will humanity.

THE MASSES AND EDUCATION TOWARD INDIVIDUALITY

The radical members of certain secret groups and societies—occupied as they are with the future leadership of humanity—hold to the conviction that any sort of deeper knowledge concerning spiritual backgrounds of earthly events must be withheld from people, because they are not mature enough for such knowledge. These radicals hold that contemporary humans cannot lead themselves. Freedom is not feasible for them; they must be led, even forced. This is indeed the opposite of what Emerson was concerned about, namely, the free independent personality. He envisioned serious danger for it. He saw that our present culture has a powerful tendency to produce collective, stereotyped human beings and that people are not aware of it, or simply do not take it seriously. Emerson saw this danger already in his century in all clarity. He was so shaken by it that he took his stand against it in harsh words. A hundred years later, this tendency has grown much stronger. And people are still not shocked into awareness by it, though there are of course exceptions. Emerson said concerning the ascendancy of the masses and those who place certain hopes in such a development:

> 'Tis pedantry to estimate nations by the census, or by square miles of land, or other than by their importance to the mind of the time. Leave this hypocritical prating about the masses. Masses are rude, lame, unmade, pernicious in their demands and influence, and need not to be flattered but to be schooled.[23]

Emerson did not wish to speak against democracy, which he valued. But he saw great danger threatening humanity and this made him say such harsh, perhaps overly harsh words.

It was the time of Michael's battle against the dragon forces. They were cast down to earth by him in order to free heaven for those who seek the spirit. Emerson did not turn against human beings but against the "spirit of the masses," against the spirit that would push humans down to the level of ego-less group beings, turning them into humans without a self of their own, human beings who in truth are no longer human. Apocalyptically speaking, this dehumanization process began in the age of "the three woes." This "spirit of the masses" is an actual Ahrimanic spirit that tries to make human beings toe the line in order to gain power over them. And this spirit opposes the future evolution of humanity.

Out of a sense of a menace threatening humanity, Emerson said of the masses: "I wish not to concede anything to them, but to tame, drill, divide and break them up, and draw individuals out of them. . . . Masses! the calamity is the masses."[24] This is a great human impulse in Emerson to develop free and ego-gifted human beings! This is the Michaelic call, the call of the Spirit of the Age, that Emerson spoke about.

His words are harsh, but people frequently do not wish to see the truth at all. They prefer living in false tranquility. Emerson was concerned with the question: How can we be saved from sliding down to a condition between human and animal? He was aware of something that was beginning to infiltrate Western culture, something like the apocalyptic beast that arises out of the abyss. Emerson felt deep concern for humanity. His efforts were directed mainly toward bringing about an awakening of the living soul, the free individuality. He believed that it is the meaning of our destiny on earth to bring the latter to birth.

> The energetic action of the times develops individualism, and the religious appear isolated. I esteem this a step in the right direction. Heaven deals with us on no representative system. Souls are saved in bundles. The Spirit saith to the man, "How is it with thee? is it well? is it ill?" For a great nature it is a happiness to escape a religious training, —religion of character is so apt to be invaded.[25]

Formed by the spirit of the masses, I can lose my ego, even through participation in religious life, such as through "religious exercises." Emerson used all the strength at his disposal to save humanity. The holy wrath that gripped him was love for his fellowmen. He spoke out of deep concern for the future destiny of humanity.

EAST AND WEST IN EMERSON

". . . In the sleep of the great heats," wrote Emerson, "there was nothing for me but to read the Vedas, the bible of the tropics, which I find I come back upon every three or four years."[26]

Emerson knew that both Eastern and Western elements were contained in his world view. He also knew that no direct bridge exists between the two. The West cannot comprehend the actual significance of the Eastern spiritual world conception. For Western, materialistically inclined people cannot admit that the spirit is a reality. Just as little can the East, having lived with its spiritual view of the world for several thousand years, grasp how human beings in the West can live with their materialism, infinite selfishness, and their dreadful struggle for existence, simply rejecting the spirit of wisdom, love, bliss, and peace. These apparently incompatible opposites actually exist in the world. Emerson sensed these opposites in himself too, but as an inwardly active person he tried to bridge the two polarities, even though it caused him difficulties. He was trained in the thinking of the West and became one of the most productive thinkers of America, something that his writings, speeches, and poems attest to. He was an independent thinker who only spoke his own mind, one who viewed any imitation as the death of the creative human being. At the same time he was an individuality in whom something unique came to manifestation, the experience of a perception that can overcome merely abstract thinking. He had discovered an open portal in himself through which the creative World Spirit could flow into his cognizing being and could penetrate him so that his thinking, speaking, and writing were ensouled by inner spiritual reality.

Two streams exist in the world. One flows out from the Tree of Knowledge, from thinking, the other from the Tree of Life, the spiritual will. The stream that gradually advanced thinking in humanity leads in our time to a new self-awareness. The human being became increasingly conscious of his own being.

In the course of time, this led to a powerful love of self, to a most egocentric attitude of mind. It isolates people in themselves and separates them from their fellow human beings. Thinking furthermore separates the individual from the soul and spirit of others and from the world. These dividing forces determine our whole life. Today, they have become antisocial and destructive. The forces of the "Tree of Knowledge" developed in the West. They brought spiritual death to the West. In the East, even though they are gradually vanishing, the forces of the "Tree of Life" have been preserved for millennia. They are the forces of a still spiritual will. In the depths of its being, the East had remained connected with the life-giving spirit, and this is still true of many people today. In the West, a person lives in wakeful day-consciousness, which in addition to great new insights, discoveries, and inventions produced powerful antisocial forces. In the East, the unconscious experience of night continues powerfully during the daytime.

In Emerson, we confront a personality who, through the dreamer-element, had preserved a powerful but not quite conscious nocturnal connection with the creative World Spirit, but through birth and education had developed Western thinking and a Western attitude of soul. In his own inner being he was able to link West and East. This way, in himself, he overcame the conflict that exists in humanity. He tried to become aware of his instincts and will-impulses, recognizing them as spiritual forces that flowed toward him out of the "night," out of the spiritual world, and bestowed on him the certainty of his connection with the spirit. In Emerson, we see a man who, in dramatic inner struggles, tried to unite the two diverse worlds of experience on a higher level. This is the same inner soul-drama that many searching young people experience today, especially in America. Hundreds of thousands of them looked for and still are looking today for a spiritual world view in the East which coincides with their *inner* impulses. Sometimes, the "Tree of Knowledge" stands in the foreground for them, sometimes, the "Tree of Life." Yet, a conflict remains in them between East and West. Emerson sought for a third way. He could not call it the "Path of Christ," but he sensed that it is a necessity for humanity's evolution to discover this third, unifying stream. He found a solution in this inner struggle only by recognizing that the cause of all separation lies in intellectual thinking, a thinking that has developed in the West and is incapable of acknowledging anything spiritual in the world. He saw the solution in his "intuitive thinking." This is able to take the East with its spirituality absolutely seriously. And it can gradually lead Western scientific thinking with its clarity and exactness into a spiritual, scientific–spiritual thinking, which in turn is capable of perceiving the creative, forming spirit in its activity in nature. It is apparent that this thinking will bring a new, higher consciousness of self and the ego, an ego-consciousness that can only be acquired through death (cutting the human being off from the spiritual world) and resurrection. This would offer the East the possibility of recognizing the value of the new development of perception in the West, whereby human beings have to pass through "materialistic death." In Emerson, this perception was the first conscious step for bridging the enormous contrasts. He was the great American who made this evident in his works. It is a step into the future. And it is admirable that this step could be taken in the nineteenth century, in an age when materialism experienced a climax in its development.

What was described above is shown in a poem by one of Emerson's friends and in two poems by himself. Poems express ideas as well as moods which make it possible for us to look more deeply into a poet's soul. The first is by Oliver

Wendell Holmes, who belonged to the "Saturday Club" that had among its members Hawthorne and Emerson. Holmes wrote his poem in memory of this club and dedicated some of the verses to Emerson:

> From his mild throng of worshippers released
> Our Concord Delphi sends its chosen priest,
> Prophet or poet, mystic, sage or seer
> By every title always welcome here.
> Why that ethereal spirit's frame describe?
> You know the race-marks of the Brahmin tribe—
> The spare, slight form, the sloping shoulders' droop,
> The calm scholastic mien, the clerky stoop.
> The lines of thought, the sharpened features wear
> Carved by the edge of keen New England air.
> Where in the realm of thought, whose air is song,
> Does he, the Buddha of the West, belong?
> He seems a winged Franklin, sweetly wise,
> Born to unlock the secrets of the skies.[27]

Holmes hardly intended to equate Emerson with Buddha, but he pointed to the impression that Emerson made on many of his friends. The poet connected the path of Buddha, who opened a new way to the spirit for human beings, with what Emerson indicated as a path to perceive the spirit through intuitive thinking. Holmes appears to underline this once more in the last line of the poem, when he says that Emerson was born to unveil the secrets of heaven to human beings. The path of the Buddha is an ancient one; Emerson's path begins to be visible today. Emerson believed that eventually, when his path would be developed further, it could unite West with East, even as he had for himself. But this is only possible when the West, with fruits of clear scientific thinking and its will to change the *earth,* can arrive at an acknowledgment of the Creator Spirit in the world. Emerson wrote:

The rounded world is fair to see,
Nine times folded in mystery:
Though baffled seers cannot impart
The secret of its laboring heart,
Throb thine with Nature's throbbing breast,
And all is clear from east to west.
Spirit that lurks each form within
Beckons to spirit of its kin;
Self-kindled every atom glows,
And hints the future which it owes.[28]

Another of his poems shows how Emerson could experience the spirit of the East as could only few Europeans and Americans of his time. The poem moreover demonstrates that a spiritual view born in the Occident can create a bridge between East and West. Anybody who is somewhat familiar with Eastern spiritual life readily recognizes the authenticity of the experience in this poem:

Brahma

If the red slayer think he slays,
Or if the slain thinks he is slain,
They know not well the subtle ways
I keep, and pass, and turn again.

Far or forgot to me is near;
Shadow and sunlight are the same;
The vanished gods to me appear;
And one to me are shame and fame.

They reckon ill who leave me out;
When me they fly, I am the wings;
I am the doubter and the doubt,
And I the hymn the Brahmin sings.

The strong gods pine for my abode,
And pine in vain the sacred Seven;

But thou, meek lover of the good!
Find me, and turn thy back on heaven.[29]

This poem shows clearly how deeply Emerson penetrated into an understanding of Eastern wisdom.

EMERSON AND THE YOUNGER GENERATION

Emerson searched for people in his age who could recognize the danger that threatened to extinguish the self. He looked for those with an inner flexibility of thinking, a warm heart, and the will to transform their age into a new era of freely developing individualism. He found these qualities only among the younger generation. He saw great possibilities in the young people, but also the difficulties that they experienced in this period of the growing materialistic view of the human being and the world. This caused him to say: "So many promising youths, and never a finished man!"[30]

What did Emerson refer to when he spoke of human instincts he had to "follow to the end?" All instincts belong to the sphere of the will; they impel a person to action. But these instinctive powers of will work initially purely as unconscious, natural forces, not as the free, personal will of an individual. All creative potential and all faculties and hopes lie in this instinctive sphere of will. If we cannot recognize them, they fade and vanish. But when we do behold them, we can awaken them to full, conscious life. Emerson was aware of the fact that only intuitive thinking can perceive and develop these deeper faculties.

How can we attain intuitive thinking? Emerson described it as follows:

> You have first an instinct, then an opinion, then a knowledge, as the plant has root, bud and fruit. Trust

the instinct to the end, though you can render no reason. It is vain to hurry it. By trusting it to the end, it
shall ripen into truth and you shall know why you
believe.[31]

With these words Emerson meant to say that we can recognize the growing instincts in ourselves if we have patience
and perseverance. If we can wait, we will observe the inner
creative workings of the spirit in our impulses. We will perceive that the forces within, the powers of the will, are part of
the Creative Spirit of the Universe, the Spirit with whom we
are united every night. If we unite in this way through inner
knowledge with the Creative Spirit of the World, we can
strengthen the inner forces, and the spiritual human character within will grow.

Out of such a development, love for our fellow human
beings can arise, for we become conscious of our common spiritual origin. Furthermore, out of this springs true love for
nature, because she too is a manifestation of the Creator
Spirit. Emerson was aware of how dangerous it is when
humans lose the heart forces. He knew that humanity must
develop these heart forces anew and in full consciousness, for
they are healing powers. ". . . the remedy for all blunders, the
cure of blindness, the cure of crime is love." For Emerson,
love was something of great significance. He wrote: "'As much
love, so much mind,' said the Latin proverb."[32]

Spiritual science, knowledge of the spirit, turns into love,
if we incorporate and digest it. When John, as he relates in
Revelation, dwelt in the spiritual world, he heard a voice from
heaven that commanded him to receive an open book from the
hand of an Angel. He then approached the Angel who gave
him the book which contained the wisdom of the world. And
the Angel said to John: "Take the book and eat!" He did not

say: "Take it and read it," but, "Take it and *eat* it, digest it, turn it into your flesh and blood so that wisdom may be transformed into life and love." Spirit can be transformed into new, creative perception, into life. It can be transformed into the heart's creative power, into love, and new faculties can be attained in this way. Then nature begins to speak to human being. This in turn produces a sense for beauty. If beauty and art are not experienced, life becomes colorless, drab, and gray; we turn into abstract, arid thinkers or blind doers. Only if we unite ourselves with the Spirit of the World can we develop living thinking, creative feeling, and powerful, self-sacrificing will. This is because the Spirit of the World Itself works out of the forces of wisdom, beauty, and love.

Emerson was open to the beauty of the world. He believed that young people cannot live without beauty. He said:

> And here let us examine a little nearer the nature of that influence which is thus potent over the human youth. Beauty, whose revelation to man we now celebrate, welcome as the sun wherever it pleases to shine, which pleases everybody with it and with themselves, seems sufficient to itself.[33]

Emerson believed that young people who exercise their sense of beauty can slowly develop the creative power of a true artist. He doubted that the older, materialistically educated generation—of course, with some exceptions—could still transform their thinking, feeling, and willing towards the spirit. He believed that the younger generation, as long as it was not devoured by the power of materialism, could achieve this. Concerning the older generation of his time, a generation that thought it was pursuing the correct direction in life and had adapted well to the circumstances of their time, he wrote:

> The Americans have many virtues, but they have not Faith and Hope. I know no two words whose meaning is more lost sight of. We use these words as if they were as obsolete as Selah and Amen. . . . The Americans have little faith. They rely on the power of a dollar; they are deaf to a sentiment. They think you may talk the north wind down as easily as raise society; and no class more faithless than the scholar or intellectual men.[34]

A new faith and a new hope can develop from the ideas of a new spiritual view. This could lead the slumbering faculties in human souls to an awakening. When Emerson looked at the deeper nature of young people, he beheld the promising faculties that each brought down to earth. He saw great possibilities that could bring about a new future. This gladdened him and he saw ways to develop them. But when he observed materialistic people, he was afraid. With a heavy heart, he had to tell himself:

> . . . Thousands of young men as hopeful now crowding to the barriers for the career do not see, that if the single man plant himself indomitably on his instincts, and there abide, the huge world will come round to him.[35]

It was his hope that the young generation of his time could achieve something for a spiritually viewed America. He repeatedly appealed to the young, and pointed out that they were living in an age of significant transition, at the beginning of a new century in American history. Something new would have to come to birth, beginning with the insight that in each and every person slumber hidden forces that are intended to be developed in order to replace the old. He hoped the young would comprehend his appeals: "I call upon you, young men, to obey your heart and be the nobility of this land."[36] It becomes evident how strongly his hope was focused on the younger generation: "I call upon you, young men, to obey your heart and be the pioneers of this land."[36]

EMERSON'S EXPECTATION REGARDING RESEARCHERS OF SUPERSENSIBLE WORLDS

Emerson was a prolific writer more than a century ago. Even though what he wrote in his day was true, ongoing evolution always takes up what was sewn at a particular age and brings it to blossom and fruit later on. Emerson knew this and often spoke of what was to come in the future. When Emerson died in 1882, Rudolf Steiner, as was mentioned, was twenty-one years old. He studied Goethe's natural-scientific works and later worked for seven years in the Goethe-Schiller Archive. Emerson was born in 1803 and was twenty-nine years old when Goethe died in 1832. This was an important year for Emerson, for he decided to leave the office of minister of the Unitarian Church in Boston. He did this because he was no longer in a position to tolerate the old traditions and frequently narrow views of the church. From this time on, he developed his own philosophy which, its uniqueness notwithstanding, resembles that of Goethe. One can sense the inner connection that existed between these two important personalities. Emerson developed profound appreciation for Goethe's scientific contributions, particularly in regard to Goethe's idea of the primal plant, the "Urpflanze." Emerson furthermore felt drawn to Goethe's other writings, his poems, and in particular his dramatic work, "Faust." Although he could be crit-

ical of Goethe, he nevertheless agreed with his basic principles.

There is an unbroken, external, historical line that leads
from Goethe to Emerson's life, and from Emerson to Rudolf
Steiner.   In addition, there is a *continuous inner line*.
Emerson and Rudolf Steiner are both connected with Goethe's
ideas and his works.   Rudolf Steiner demonstrated how
Anthroposophy advances Goethe's ideas further.   Since
Emerson's work had its source in the same spirit of idealism
as did Goethe's—strictly speaking, "Realistic Idealism"—we
can discern a profound connection between Emerson and
Rudolf Steiner. Emerson tried hard to apply his thoughts to
practical life so as to change human life and destiny on earth.
He emphasized active will and tried to change existing culture
with the aid of his spiritual thoughts, thoughts that were
imbued with a creative, ennobled will force. He said:

> I believe that intellect and ethics are the same
> being. I believe the more wise man is, the more in an
> astonishing way will appear to him the compensation
> between nature and ethic.[32]

We must develop a thinking entirely different from that of
today in order to find it credible that intellect and ethics flow
from one and the same source. It is unthinkable that traditional thinking can ever unite nature and ethics.

In many lectures, Rudolf Steiner describes the tragic division between thinking and morality, the cause of which is our
"head-thinking" that has developed since the 15th century.
This division is the reason for the destructive tendencies and
moral decay of our civilization, predicted by Rudolf Steiner
more than seventy years ago. A spiritual thinking can bridge
this chasm and can unite morality and thinking because, seen

spiritually, both come from the same source. The cosmos is not a machine but a world with a visible body, permeated by the actively working justice of the Creator Spirit. Unless we recognize this truth, we will not be able to do anything to stem the tides of destruction, chaos, and moral decay. On the contrary, they will grow stronger and stronger.

A spiritual thinking grasps the number "three" in the human being, nature, and the cosmos in a new way. Emerson had a special relationship to this number. He often spoke of the three soul forces of thinking, feeling, and willing, for example as follows:

> Insight is not will, nor is affection will. Perception is cold, and goodness dies in wishes. . . . There must be a fusion of these two to generate the energy of will.[37]

He tried to relate these three soul forces with the three world forces in the cosmos:

> For the Universe has three children, born at one time, which reappear under different names in every system of thought, whether they be called cause, operation and effect; or, more poetically, Jove, Pluto, Neptune; or, theologically, the Father, the Spirit and the Son; but which we will call here the Knower, the Doer and the Sayer. These stand respectively for the love of truth, for the love of good, and for the love of beauty. These three are equal. Each is that which he is, essentially, so that he cannot be surmounted or analyzed, and each of these three has the power of the others latent in him and his own, patent.[38]

In these words by Emerson, an amazing understanding of the significance of the number three, of its human and cosmic aspects, comes to light. This understanding leads one to view the single human being as well as the whole of humanity in their threefoldness—the forces of thinking, feeling, and willing—or science, beauty (art), and morality—or West, East, Middle. Despite their differences, says Emerson, each of these three latently contain the forces of the others, ready to be developed.

Rudolf Steiner always regarded the human being in a threefold way. He linked the three main soul forces in the human being—thinking, feeling, willing—to the three systems in the physical body: the nerve–sense system as the bearer of our thinking and consciousness, the rhythmic system with the rhythm of inhaling and exhaling and the rhythmic pulsation of the blood as the bearer of feeling, the metabolic-limb system as the bearer of the will forces.

In his book, *Riddles of the Soul*, Rudolf Steiner wrote in 1917 for the first time about this threefoldness. He demonstrated that, even though thinking takes place mainly in the head, an attentive observer can also find feeling and will concealed there; or thinking and will hidden in the heart forces, and thinking and feeling latent in the will organism.[39]

When Rudolf Steiner referred to the world situation, he proceeded from a threefold viewpoint as well: from the East (Asia), from the Middle (Europe), and from the West (America). He spoke of the East as linked with spirit (thinking); Europe as connected with the soul forces (feeling, and contained in feeling, the maturing ego); America as linked with the forces of will that work out of the physical body, the metabolic-limb system. Through his spiritual research, Rudolf Steiner recognized that, from each of these parts of the world, a different, important, spiritual capacity arises, but that each nonetheless contains the other two within itself. He depicted this in words similar to those of Emerson. He spoke of the three branches of culture: science, art and religion (or ethics). For the social life he described the three members of the social organism: the life of culture and education; the life of rights and laws; the economic life.

Thus, we can become aware of the working of the "three" in the threefold human being, in the threefold social organism, and in the threefold geographic condition, and finally, viewed cosmically, in the threefoldness of Father, Son, and Holy Spirit.

Anthroposophy finds many related thoughts in Emerson's world view. Many spiritual ideas, that meanwhile have matured in the 20th century, can only continue to grow if human beings develop a higher consciousness; a thinking that grows more and more active and alive inwardly and can slowly pass over into a new "thinking clairvoyance," one that rises in three levels of inner development to Imagination, Inspiration, and Intuition. By means of this new form of spiritual effort, people can prepare themselves step by step with the clarity of scientific insight for a spiritual exploration of the supersensible worlds.

The new faculty of clairvoyance originates in the transformation of our present-day intellect into a higher faculty of thinking (of Imagination). It is important to remember that a new spiritual perception is the fruit of modern thinking. This is the basis of the path of spiritual science. At the end of his essay, "The Oversoul," Emerson writes:

> More and more the surges of everlasting nature enter into me, and I become public and human in my regards and actions. So I come to live in thoughts, and act with energies which are immortal. . . . I am somehow receptive of the great soul, and thereby I do overlook the sun and the stars and feel them to be the fair accidents and effects which change and pass. . . . Thus revering the soul, and learning, as the ancient said,

that "its beauty is immense," man will come to see that the world is the perennial miracle which the soul worketh, and be less astonished at particular wonders; he will learn that there is no profane history; that all history is sacred; that the universe is represented in an atom, in a moment of time. He will weave no longer a spotted life of shreds and patches, but he will live with a divine unity. He will cease from what is base and frivolous in his life and be content with all places and with any service he can render.[40]

We have to note that Emerson never forgets the element of thought. He not only wished to feel nature but also to have thoughts about it, thoughts of a spiritual-cosmic kind. He wished to live in thoughts and act out of spiritual capacities. Emerson believed that, in the future, a number of people will begin to explore the spiritual world. This becomes evident in numerous writings, in the essays and his lectures, for example in the introduction to his work, *Representative Men*.

When those will emerge who know about the true standard of values, the determination of value of the common marks of honour will sink down to the stand of cooks and confectioners. The genius is the scientist or geographer for the supersensible regions and will design a map of the new supersensible areas. But we, who become acquainted thereby with new areas of creation, lost something of our former admiration. . . . Then he appears as an exponent of vaster mind and will. The opaque self becomes transparent with the light of the First Cause.[41]

Emerson was convinced that, in time to come, people with developed Western scientific thinking will become researchers of the supersensible world and that they will inform us about spheres, beings, and forces of the higher worlds, just as scientists instruct people about the realms they have explored. This is also the way of Anthroposophy, and, for this reason, it is spiritual science. Emerson foretold the future; Anthroposophy fulfills his hopes.

Emerson stated: "We owe man a higher support than food and fire. We owe man—The Man." Anthroposophy means, "wisdom of man." This unveils its deepest impulse, namely, to bring the true Human Being to the human being. This is the most significant impulse in the world. In Emerson lived a sort of "invisible Anthroposophy," concerning which Rudolf Steiner said that it dwells in America in a "wooden" manner, as yet not in a living one. But he stated that it would come alive one day and would be able to reveal something new and significant. This is not possible without the help of the true Central European spirit. And this insight contains the challenge for Europe and America to work together in the spiritual realm.

BIOGRAPHY OF EMERSON

(From the Epilogue of *Ralph Waldo Emerson, Essays*, translated and published by Harald Kiczka, Diogenes Verlag, Zürich, 1982.)

Ralph Waldo Emerson was born on May 25, 1803 in an old parsonage in Boston. Prior to his father, seven generations of his forefathers had been clergymen. The father's early death brought material hardship to the mother, Ruth Haskins Emerson, but with the help of the Puritanical aunt, Mary Moody Emerson, she made it possible for her children to attend school. The aunt's stern motto: "Always do what you fear to do!" exerted strong pressure on the youngsters. Already as children, Ralph Waldo and his four brothers had to read the Greek and Roman philosophers. While the father had complained in 1806 that Ralph Waldo was having a hard time reading and writing, the aunt urged the children to read Plato in the evening, wrapped in wool blankets in the cold room. Since that time, Plato was linked in Emerson's memory with the smell of this wool blanket. The voluminous correspondence between the aunt and the child, who wrote poems as early as age 10, bears witness to the powerful, lasting impression she made on him. In 1813, Ralph Waldo began to attend the Boston Latin School, but hardly excelled in his scholastic performance. In 1817, he was accepted into Harvard. Emerson ran errands for the president of the university and in turn received free room and board. This additional work left little time for his studies. During the winter months, he worked as a manservant in the school of his uncle, Samuel Ripley, while he taught in the private school of his brother William during the summer months.

All in all, Emerson wrote of his school years that he gained little from them, except for the strong effect exerted by the high qualifications of his professors in modern languages, Greek, and English composition. His affiliation and work with a literary club, the "Pythologian Club," gave him great pleasure. He received a prize for Free Speech and two most coveted Bowdoin prizes for his essays, "The Character of Socrates," and "The Present State of Ethical Philosophy." He started to keep a diary in 1820. This remained his habit for the following fifty years. Many of the thoughts contained in his essays, lectures, and poems are found in his diaries in the form of aphorisms. "Pay so much attention to the visits that truth pays to your spirit that you will note them down," became his motto.

In conversing with himself, young Emerson was occupied with themes on religion. In the years 1825 to 1833, this reached a culmination in his sermons. Then followed the *Early Lectures*, given before a scientifically oriented audience at the university. The content of the lectures appealed to the listeners' interest. Following his years of study, he became a teacher, and later the principal, at his brother's school. But soon after, in 1825, he closed this school and decided to start his training as a minister at Cambridge Divinity School. He received his approbation as a pastor in 1829. Then followed extensive journeys preaching all over the eastern United States. He accepted a position as preacher at the Boston

Unitarian Church in 1829. His marriage to Louisa Tucker ended after a year and a half in 1832, due to her untimely death. He resigned his clerical office the same year, because it became impossible for him to conduct the ritual, particularly the transubstantiation, with complete presence of mind. The decision to leave the priesthood was not an easy one for him, as evidenced by many letters and diary entries. Later he wrote: "Sometimes I think it is necessary to give up the priesthood in order to be a good priest." This change in his outward position reflects a deep inner crisis, for eight years earlier he had chosen this profession following careful consideration.

Viewed outwardly, his leaving the pastoral office was an expression of this life crisis. Emerson wrote: "One who wants to be a man must be a nonconformist. In the end, nothing is sacred except the inviolability of your own spirit." The question of conscience, which had become torturous for him, drove the perplexed man into the solitary mountainous world of New Hampshire to Ethan Crawford, to where "life is thought over once more."

His first trip to Europe occurred during this time of crisis. The journey must be seen from this viewpoint: He had departed in order to find teachers. In Italy he looked up Walter Savage Landor whom he greatly esteemed. In France he was the guest of Lafayette. Wordsworth, Carlyle, John Stuart Mill, and Samuel Taylor Coleridge led him to England. One could say that his years of study were followed by his years of travel. It fits this picture that, after his return, he posed the question: Where and how should I live? He decided on the small town of Concord which, in American history, is honored as the bastion against the advancing British army in 1775.

Situated not far from Boston and founded by one of Emerson's ancestors, Concord was destined to become the cultural center of America in the years from 1830 to the eighties

of that century. Emerson had settled in Concord in 1833. Famous literary figures followed him. Philosophers established their schools here and poets wrote their world-famous works. There, we find Amos Bronson Alcott, the educator-reformer; Henry David Thoreau, the man of nonviolent resistance and civil disobedience; Nathaniel Hawthorne, author of darkly ominous novels; and Margaret Fuller, Goethe-admirer and fighter for equal rights for women.

Concord was a cultural center close to economically oriented Boston. In the surroundings of Concord, reformers of social issues gathered to realize their ideas in the "Brook Farm Experiment" and the "Fruitland Community." These ideas of a world conception that had come to realization in the surroundings of Emerson were supposed to contribute to an overcoming of the materialism of the age. They were an essential ingredient of the conception of nature as represented by Emerson. In fact, one has to see in Emerson the father, the protector of all these efforts and aims. He himself did not participate in the active efforts but followed them with keen interest.

One has to realize that demands for a cultural life were increasingly heard in this age. As early as 1836, in the introduction to his book, *Nature*, Emerson spoke of the idea, which in 1837 was to become the subject of his famous address, "The American Scholar." "Let us demand our own works, laws and our own form of worship!"

In his "Divinity School Address" of 1838 to the graduating classes of theology students, he declared that the church as an institution was dead and that the office of the priest was obsolete. He called for independence of scientists from the church, and for a new revelation appropriate to the age. Little applause was subsequently heard from the ranks of the ministry, but his words were received with stormy acclaim by the

young students. After these provocations, Emerson had to bury his hopes for an academic career. In Harvard, he was to be *persona non grata* for the next 30 years. Already in 1836, he had made enemies with his work *Nature*, even though he had initially published it anonymously. But now he had to find another stage for his lectures, because many pulpits also remained inaccessible to him. He had become controversial.

Across the whole country, so-called lyceums had been established. They were small halls in libraries or schools. Lecturers from all over gathered there for lively exchanges. These "platforms" were study sites in addition to universities and colleges. Emerson accepted invitations to many large cities, traveled as far as San Francisco, and met with the Hegelians of St. Louis.

Together with Margaret Fuller, he published the magazine, *The Dial* from 1840 to 1844. It grew to be *the* literary journal for the people around Emerson. As early as 1839, Margaret Fuller had translated and published Eckermann's *Conversations with Goethe*, and had been instrumental in the proliferation of German literature, particularly that of Bettina von Arnim and Goethe. Emerson's essays, twelve in the first series of 1841, nine in the second series of 1847, established his literary fame. His young friend, Henry Thoreau, lived for two years in Emerson's house. During this time, Emerson undertook extensive lecture tours throughout North America. In addition, he was involved as a publisher of the writings by Carlyle, among others, and he translated Dante's *Vita Nuova*. He followed an invitation to England to give lectures there. On this occasion, he again visited his friend Carlyle, became acquainted with Alfred Lord Tennyson and Charles Dickens, and visited Samuel Taylor Coleridge. Following his return, he immediately resumed his extensive lecturing activity. Now he unequivocally sided with the emancipation of slaves, just as

he had fought for the rights of the American Indians in 1835. John Brown was a guest in Emerson's home. In 1862, Abraham Lincoln was one of his listeners in Washington. Subsequently, Lincoln, the politician, and Emerson, the literary scholar, met in the White House. In these years, his literary output had almost passed its zenith. His physical energies diminished. His attempt to withdraw into the quiet of his home or the surrounding woods failed. Emerson had attained world fame. Even Harvard recognized this now. He received an honorary Doctor of Laws degree. The animosity of thirty years was symbolically ended by the appointment as overseer at Harvard. The "Sage of Concord" was visited and besieged by admirers and people who sought his advice, above all young people from all over the world.

After his house had burned down in 1872—a fire that surprised the family at night, destroyed a number of unpublished manuscripts and dealt a decisive blow to the already weak constitution of the old man—he allowed himself to be persuaded to go on yet another trip to Europe. His daughter Ellen accompanied him. They traveled to England, France and Italy, and to Egypt; and then took on the reverse route back to England. In March of 1873 in Florence, Emerson and his daughter met his friend and admirer Herman Grimm and Grimm's wife Gisela von Arnim. They had been corresponding with each other for decades. In England, he was the guest of William Gladstone, Thomas Huxley, and Max Müller. In May, he embarked on his return voyage and was jubilantly welcomed home by an enthusiastic crowd. During his absence, the visitors to Concord had rebuilt his house. When he died on April 27, 1882, he was a man whose name was known to every American.

EMERSON CHRONICLE

(From *Ralph Waldo Emerson, Essays,* translated and published by Harald Kiczka, Diogenes Verlag, Zürich, 1982.)

1803	May 25: Ralph Waldo Emerson is born to Reverend William Emerson and Ruth Haskins Emerson in Boston, Massachusetts.
1811 ff	After the father's death, the mother takes care of the five children, William, Ralph Waldo, Edward Bliss, Robert Bulkeley and Charles Chauncy. 1813-1817, Ralph Waldo attends the Boston Latin School.
1817-1821	14-year-old Ralph Waldo attends Harvard College. There, he belongs to a literary society; receives a prize for Free Speech, and two Bowdoin prizes for his essays, "The Character of Socrates" and "The Present State of Ethical Philosophy." He writes poems and starts keeping a diary, something he continues until old age. During the summer months, he teaches at the school of his brother William in Boston.
1822-1831	Following his studies, he earns his living working as a private teacher; pays off debts and helps support his mother and brother William, who is studying in Göttingen and who, during his studies in Germany, becomes acquainted with Goethe. In February of 1825, Ralph Waldo Emerson enrolls in the Divinity School at Cambridge and in October 1826 receives appro-

bation to become a preacher. An ailment of his lungs forces him to spend the winter in the South. He gives sermons in many towns there and returns to Boston in the summer of 1827. In 1829, he accepts a position as minister at the Second Unitarian Church in Boston. He marries Ellen Louisa Tucker, who, having contracted tuberculosis, dies after 18 months of marriage.

1832-1836   Ralph Waldo Emerson leaves the parsonage. The state of his health worsens once more and he does not find a new position. He travels to Europe. In Italy and France, he looks up Walter Savage Landor and Lafayette. In England, he is the guest of Samuel Taylor Coleridge and William Wordsworth; in Scotland, he visits with Thomas Carlyle, with whom he will entertain a lifelong friendship. In September 1833, he returns to America and resumes his extensive lecturing activity. Lydia Jackson becomes his second wife in 1835. They live in the famous "Old Manse" in Concord. Here, Emerson writes his first book, *Nature*, which is published three years later, in September 1836. His son Waldo is born in October 1836. A study group is established (Transcendental Club).

1837-1842   Continuation of his lecture activity in Boston and other cities in New England and New York. In 1837 he gives his, later well known, address at Harvard, "The American Scholar." In it, he demands America's cultural independence and points out the necessity of becoming culturally creative in America. He takes a stand against slavery and occupies himself in his lectures mainly with the theme, "Human Culture." Speaking to the students of the seminary in 1838, he gives "The Divinity School Address." The thoughts set forth in it meet with rejection by many of the school's instructors. Emerson can no longer count on an academic career. In 1840, Margaret Fuller puts out the magazine, *The Dial,* which becomes the voice of the circle of people around Emerson. In 1839, she translates and publishes Eckermann's *Conversations with Goethe*, three years later the correspondence between Miss Günderode and Bettina von Arnim. In 1842, Emerson becomes publisher of *The Dial.* Births of daughters Ellen (1839) and Edith (1842). In 1841 he publishes the first series of his *Essays*, with 12 articles, and the treatise, "The Method of Nature." Henry David Thoreau lives for two years in Emerson's house. Emerson's son Waldo dies in 1842. The lecture themes during this span of time are: "Speech on American Slavery," ten lectures with the theme, "Human Culture," "Address on War," "Divinity School Address," the lecture cycles, "Human Life" and "The Present Age;" beginning of the lecture cycle, "The Times." In addition, poems, essays, treatises, and reviews appeared frequently in various American magazines.

1843-1846   His lecturing activity leads him to Philadelphia, Baltimore, and Washington. He translates Dante's *Vita Nuova* and publishes his second series of *Essays* with nine articles. His friend

Thoreau lives in a hut at Walden Pond and writes his main work, "Walden." Emerson supports the social reformers, who hope to realize their ideas in "Brook Farm" (George Ripley) and "Fruitlands" (Amos Bronson Alcott). He does not participate in their endeavors. In 1846, he publishes his first volume of poems. He occupies himself in lectures with the problem of slavery: "The Young American," "Address on Emancipation in the British West Indies," "The Scholar," and a series of seven lectures about "Representative Men."

1847-1854 He follows Alexander Ireland's invitation to give lectures in England. Again he looks up Carlyle and Wordsworth and becomes acquainted with Alfred Tennyson and Charles Dickens. After his stay in Paris he returns in 1848 to Concord, where he immediately takes up his lecturing activity again. In 1849, he publishes his fifth book, *Nature, Addresses and Lectures*, and *Representative Men* in 1850. Margaret Fuller-Ossoli loses her life in a shipwreck. His mother dies in 1853. He gives lectures in New York, Ohio, Illinois, Missouri, Michigan, and Wisconsin. The subjects range from an "Address Against the 'Fugitive Slave Law'," which forbids any American from offering shelter to escaping slaves, to his lecture series, "Conduct of Life." In 1852, he writes a *Biography of Margaret Fuller* with James Freeman Clarke and William Henry Channing.

1855-1860 Emerson gives lectures in New England, New

York, Canada, and many of the western states. Again and again, through word and deed, he intercedes for the movement to free the slaves. In 1856 he publishes his *English Traits*, and in 1860, *The Conduct of Life*. During these years, he begins the correspondence with Herman Grimm and Frau Gisela von Arnim, who later corresponds with Emerson's daughter, Ellen. The freedom fighter, John Brown, repeatedly visits Concord and is the guest of Frank Sanborn and Emerson. John Brown gives a talk at the city hall of Concord and, from there, organizes shelters and points of support for slaves escaping to Canada. In 1859, John Brown is sentenced to death and hanged. During this time, Emerson gives lectures to a Women's Rights Convention in Boston, his "Anti-Slavery Address," in 1855; six philosophical lectures in Boston; a lecture cycle, "Manners and Art," in 1859, and many others.

1861-1865   In Washington, Abraham Lincoln is among his listeners. The encounter between Emerson and Lincoln takes place in Washington in 1862. During this year, his much younger friend, Henry David Thoreau, dies. Emerson organizes the celebrations for the Emancipation Proclamation in Boston. In 1864, he holds a series of lectures, "Social Aims," and gives others as well.

1866-1871   Publication in 1867 of a volume of poems, *May-Day and Other Pieces*. A new edition of his prose writings in six volumes comes out in 1870. Publication of new essays in *Society and*

Solitude. He writes an introduction for Plutarch's *Moralia.* His lecturing activity now extends to San Francisco. In 1870, he gives his lecture series, "The Natural History of Intellect," at Harvard.

1872-1882   Following the burning of his house and his subsequent illness, he travels with his daughter Ellen to England, France, Italy, and Egypt from 1872 to 1873. He meets Herman Grimm in Florence. His return to Concord is celebrated with many honors being bestowed on him. His weakening state of health forces him to curtail his lecturing activity. His daughter Ellen and his friend and later biographer, John Cabot, edit his lectures and publish some of them as *Letters and Social Aims* in 1875. Together with Amos Bronson Alcott and Dr. H. K. Jones, Emerson establishes the "Concord School of Philosophy," in which he gives lectures and addresses right up to the time of his death.

1882   On April 27, Ralph Waldo Emerson dies of pneumonia in his home in Concord.

CORRESPONDENCE
BETWEEN EMERSON AND HERMAN GRIMM
BY FRIEDRICH HIEBEL

Das Goetheanum,
48th annual series, #34 of August 24, 1969

We catch glimpses of the element of destiny that prevailed between Emerson and Grimm in the correspondence which, sparse as it may be, emerges all the more significantly, its fragmentary briefness notwithstanding.

Herman Grimm bequeathed the letters he exchanged with Emerson to the Goethe-Schiller Archive in Weimar. Most likely, Rudolf Steiner also gained access to these documents during the seven years he stayed in Weimar working in the Archive. Subsequently, his destiny-perceptive vision of insight probably rested on the creative friendship of these two spirits, men who outwardly were separated by an ocean, but united by a common clarion call for culture.

Three days prior to his death, Herman Grimm received a visit by the American writer, Frederick William Holls, whom he gave permission to publish this correspondence in America. Grimm gave Holls a letter addressed to the director of the Archive, Bernhard Suphan. Shortly afterwards, when Holls arrived in Weimar, he was informed by Suphan of Herman Grimm's sudden death. The charge to publish the correspondence is therefore part of the last bequest by the great essayist and scholar of art. Two years after his death, *Correspondence Between Ralph Waldo Emerson and Herman Grimm* (edited by Frederick William Holls, Boston & New

York, 1903) appeared in print. It was a thin little volume, but of rare significance as a spiritual and historical message.

Since Grimm's letters were written in German, they came out in English translation simultaneously. Emerson's letters, on the other hand, were only published in the original English text. The correspondence consists of twelve messages. With long intervals in between, they were exchanged from 1856 to 1871. A few of Emerson's letters were also addressed to Gisela von Arnim, later Grimm's wife.

The first letter of this small collection, mailed by the twenty-eight-year old Grimm from Berlin on April 5, 1856 to the fifty-three-year old Emerson in Concord, is particularly moving because of the expression of an immediate meeting of minds despite the spatial distance and linguistic limitations:

> A year ago I became acquainted with your writings. Since then I have read them again and again with renewed admiration.

This is how Grimm began in unrestrained praise, confessing furthermore to an intimate sense of being linked in spirit with Emerson:

> Everywhere, I seem to rediscover my own most secret thoughts, even the words in which I would most likely have wanted to express them.

It is a rediscovery of his own being in experiencing the other. It makes him continue in the following sentences:

> Of all the writers of our time, it seems to me that you understand the genius of the age most profoundly and feel our future the most clearly. It makes me happy to be able to tell you this.

This letter was not entrusted to the sea-mail of those days. It was given personally to a friend, A. W. Thayer, who was returning to America. More than two years passed before Emerson decided on a reply to Grimm from Concord, when Thayer, once more on a European journey, forwarded the letter along with copies of all his books to Grimm.

Emerson's letter to his German admirer, who in age could have been his son, still has a sound of temporizing detachment. After apologies for the much delayed confirmation of the letter's receipt, Emerson asserted that he had read with interest Grimm's poetical works. The essay about Shakespeare, translated by Grimm from *Representative Men*, caused Emerson to remark that he was proud to have been introduced to Berlin under such a good omen. He added that he was no less pleased to have read his own words in the German language. In conclusion, he expressed the hope to welcome Grimm one day in his home in America. He also mentioned that he felt he was at an age when one prefers to remain in one place. At the same time, he wrote to Gisela von Arnim, Bettina's daughter, who subsequently married Grimm, thanked her for the books that had been sent to him, and remembered her famous mother with due respect.

The fourth letter is once more penned by Emerson. This leads to the assumption that an answer by Grimm had been lost, for it would make no sense that the German friend did not gratefully acknowledge receipt of all of Emerson's books. The letter of July 9, 1858 from Concord was written under the immediate impression of his having read the Michelangelo essay. Emerson's style was becoming noticeably warmer. The previous paternalistically expressed joy over Grimm's translation into German now made way for the voice of a friend, who declared without reservation that he would stand up for Grimm and quote him as much as possible in lectures and essays. Again, he encouraged Grimm to come to America:

"You and I shall not fear to meet, or to be silent." In the end, he added with genuine modesty:

> It is to be expected that such freedom of thoughts, as is peculiar of me, becomes a nuisance for an Englishman or a clergyman in America. But I ascribe this same freedom to you Germans from habit. It definitely is part of Goethe, Schiller, and Novalis.

Herman Grimm replied to this letter of July 9, 1859 more than a year later, on October 25, 1860, after he had married Gisela von Arnim. In the meantime, Bettina and his father, Wilhelm Grimm, had died.

> I would only like to tell you how often I have opened your books during this time and found becalming consolation in them. You write that everyone who reads your words has to think that you had thought of him alone—only too powerfully does one sense the love you harbor for all human beings—one thinks it is impossible that you did not refer to merely a few privileged ones, and one counts oneself among them. What good fortune it is for a country to possess a man such as you! When I think of America, I think of you, and America thus seems to me to be the foremost country on earth. You know well, I would not say this if it were not in fact my innermost conviction. The course of things and events appears to me like the rhythm of a beautiful poem when I read your words, and the basest matter dissolves in necessary beauty through your observation. . . . I have attempted to write my book on Michel Angelo in agreement with your views, every page in such a way that it would stand the test if I were to read it to you.

In the end he asked Emerson critically to evaluate the first part of his book on Michelangelo so that his second vol-

ume might profit from it. Emerson's reply—the most voluminous letter of the correspondence—followed eight months
later, on June 27, 1861. After customary apologies for yet
another long pause, he wrote concerning the Michelangelo
book:

> The book is a treasure . . . it contains research,
> method, and daylight. . . . I am proud of my friend and
> his accomplishments. . . . Thank you always for this
> precious fruit you sent me across the ocean.

He expressed the hope that Grimm could speak English
when they would meet, for Emerson would probably never be
capable of speaking the German language. "But I feel
assuaged that, owing to your greater scholarliness, you and I
will one of these days be able to have a long conversation in
English."

The American Civil War, which had broken out at that
time, interrupted the exchange of letters for years. Emerson's
next letter to Grimm from Concord on April 14, 1867 arrived
almost six years later. It was handed over to William James,
the philosopher, who later on was to become famous. Then he
was living in Germany as a medical student. Again, half a
year went by before Herman Grimm answered. On October
19, 1867, he wrote from Berlin:

> Esteemed Sir and Friend. . . . I read your books
> over and over again; your letters made me happy and
> nothing pleased me more than to hear somebody tell
> me something of you. I could not name anybody I
> would like to know except you. If I were not afraid of
> the voyage on account of my wife, I would have come
> long ago. Alas, she would not be able to tolerate the
> voyage. . . . Mr. James has arrived here and we like

him very much. Tomorrow night, at our house, he will meet Joachim, the famous violinist, who is also my best friend and moreover the one who, together with me, was the first in Germany to become acquainted with your thoughts to their full import. Joachim and I read your works at a time in Germany when, except for us, probably nobody knew them. Now, of course, many know them and learn to know them better all the time.

Three additional brief letters by Emerson to Herman Grimm are included in the collection. Each time they were entrusted to a visiting friend, the last one, of December 18, 1871, to his son Edward. On this occasion, Emerson wrote:

I take this occasion to tell you that, even though I have a very bad habit of not writing letters, the finest books and writings from your hand arrived here. They were read by me carefully and to my greatest benefit.

This concludes the collection that Holls copied in the Goethe-Schiller Archive in Weimar and then published in America. A personal meeting between the two finally came about; it occurred neither in America nor in Germany but in Florence in the spring of 1873. Grimm, who shortly before this had been nominated professor of Art History at the University of Berlin, was forty-five years old. Emerson was seventy and was traveling in the company of his daughter Ellen from Rome to Florence. It is moving to read what Herman Grimm (in the third series of his fifteen essays) admitted concerning this significant encounter in Italy. It seemed to him as if he had become acquainted with Emerson already in his youth.

This meeting with the seventy-year-old Emerson was not the beginning of something new. It became the final point of a process. Young Grimm had discovered Emerson's essays at age twenty-seven. A year later the twenty-eight-year-old wrote that he felt he had rediscovered his own, most secret thoughts, "even the words in which I would most likely have wanted to express them." Four years later, he called across the ocean in his letter to Emerson: "When I think of America, I think of you, and America thus seems to me to be the foremost country on earth." Every page in his Michelangelo book was to stand the test of being read by Emerson with approval. And in 1867, the almost forty-year-old Grimm wrote that he would not know who to name whom he would wish to meet aside from Emerson. Grimm always regarded Emerson as a disciple would the teacher who is older than he by one generation. Emerson's replies, only gradually lost their cool restraint and polite formality, until, in 1861, he called the Michelangelo book a treasure that he acknowledged without reservation.

During his years in Weimar, Rudolf Steiner's attention was most likely directed to this correspondence as well, for Herman Grimm belonged to the few individuals whom he genuinely admired. Decades later, on April 23, 1924, Rudolf Steiner gave a lecture in which he presented significant insights into the destiny relationship existing between Emerson and Grimm. The arc of the spirit-encounter Rudolf Steiner himself had had with Herman Grimm itself fatefully came full circle. At the same time, the light he threw on the relationship of the two individuals illuminated the spiritual-historical background of history, biography, and essayistics. The land where their relationship originated was Italy in the twilight-radiance of Roman Antiquity and the early dawn of Tuscan Renaissance.

Carl Stegmann
Ca. 1976

Christine Stegmann
Ca. 1976

CARL STEGMANN

March 15, 1897–February 16, 1996

Carl Friedrich Heinrich Stegmann's life spanned nearly a hundred years and one of the most intense world-changing centuries in human history. He was awake to his time with spiritual awareness, his vision on the future, his deeds of social action ever in the present.

His fiery spirit manifested in Carl's countenance, a face chiseled from strength, powerful brow, nose, and chin, a large listening ear, a keen and piercing glance. His inner seeing was eagle-like as well, high, far, and sun-filled. He cast that spiritual vision across America and hoped that multitudes would come to share it.

Carl was born with the dawn of the Light Age (1899), in the seacoast town of Kiel, Germany. He was the oldest child of three in his father's second family (seven in all). His father worked as a superintendent on the docks. Carl described gazing out on the harbor as a child and to the sea whose many moods he knew—where the horizon blended with the endlessness of the blue skies, where heaven and earth merge and overcome all boundaries of time and place. As he watched ships coming from exotic ports around the world, he longed to travel with them, but most of all to go to the fabled land of America. Seven decades later that dream was realized when Carl and his wife Christine came to live in California, joining their destiny with a new land, a new language, and the people of the West.

Carl and America were made for each other. He understood the will—the deep driving soul force that brought millions to America with hope for a better life. He recognized that in this soul capacity lies tremendous spiritual power if rightly awakened. America is deeply indebted to such a champion. As Alexis de Tocqueville wrote about America with an open and discerning eye in the last century, Carl Stegmann has written his provocative work about the spiritual America in this century.

A sense of his spiritual individuality came to Carl when he nearly died as a small child. He was less than four when the family was celebrating with many others at a town gathering. Always eager for action, he climbed an old tower structure following a group of older children. He fell from a great height and lay unconcious, seriously injured. Yet he felt his spirit leaving the crumpled body to go and seek his mother who was conversing in a coffee house nearby. His mother instantly responded and rushed to his side, sustaining him through what would be a long recovery. This spiritual experience, a first of many, grounded him in spiritual reality and the truth of the higher self. Throughout his life he would exhort individuals to find themselves, to develop "the own Self," the higher individuality which can direct and shine through the lower self. One of his first publications in America was called "In Search of the Future: The Struggle for the Creative Core of Man."

Carl learned the locksmith's trade and served as a soldier through four years of World War I, experiencing firsthand the terrible suffering it caused. He made a silent vow that if he survived it he would "dedicate his life to ideas and powers which would make such cruel events impossible and would bring about peace." He was 22 when he met the work of Rudolf Steiner.

He often told how his destiny as a Christian Community priest was forged at a seemingly chance meeting with a young man asking directions of Carl as he came from the train station in Kiel. The young man was seeking individuals interested in founding an anthroposophical movement for religious ᵣenewal. They talked for hours on a grassy knoll overlooking the town and the blue Baltic sea. The man told him it would be a religious movement that not only considered those on earth, but also those across the threshold and the spiritual hierarchies. "That is when I knew I wanted to be a priest!" Carl said later. At the West-East Congress in Vienna, Carl asked Friedrich Rittelmeyer, one of the leading Protestant theologians, if individuals who were not university academics could be part of this religious movement. Given an affirmative answer, Carl became one of the forty-five priests founding a new religious movement arising out of the ashes of the First World War. They began with meetings in a stable, sleeping ten to a room on straw beds in the village, and were ultimately ordained in the beautiful white room of the first Goetheanum in Switzerland.

Carl did not come to the movement meekly. Much oppression had occurred in the name of Christianity and he could only unite himself with a cause that recognized human freedom. He disdained the "decided impotence in relation to social and practical life" characteristic of the churches he knew. He burned with questions and longing for true social change, as did many young people of his time. He called himself a "free spirit" who yearned to be a poet and dramatist. His writings, full of these issues, found their way to Rudolf Steiner. When Steiner gave the lectures for *The Younger Generation*, Carl knew his questions for young people and the future were being answered.

When Carl took a six-month course for those who wanted to work with youth, he heard people speaking of a young woman who would shortly be joining the course. "When they said her name, Christine, I felt, ' that is my wife,' " Carl related, "and then when I saw her I knew this was true." Christine was nineteen when they married; she later became a eurythmist. Theirs was a blessed union of two resolute souls with a lifelong dedication to furthering Anthroposophy. Together they had seven children, four sons and three daughters who all took up teaching or medical professions and who gave them deep fulfillment as parents. Three of their sons were called into military service in the Second World War. Only one returned. Those were years of great poverty for the family as well as imprisonment for Carl. Christine, with quintessential bravery, stood up to the Gestapo and refused an award for having a large family for the Fatherland. Their children remember being surrounded with the iron calm and fearless courage of their parents during the bombings, while others gave way to hysteria. Carl once rescued his youngest daughter from the flames of their burning home in the bombing of Mannheim.

Even while Carl dedicated himself to establishing the anthroposophical and Christian Community work in Mannheim after the war, the desire to come to America remained. Carl was 73 when he and Christine moved to California, bringing a lifetime of research about America gleaned from Steiner's statements scattered throughout his voluminous lectures.

They established a Christian Community in their home in Oakland, a busy, multicultural city near San Francisco. At an age when most people retire, Carl and Christine did not even consider retirement. They shaped each day with iron discipline: morning and evening meditation, study, research, writing, fulfilling priestly duties, and making connections with the many individuals with whom he would work. Carl did enjoy owning a car and was as formidable on the road as he was in the pulpit. They once made a memorable whirlwind trip to visit the Grand Canyon in half the time usually required!

Young people flocked around them both. Carl was a patriarch such as few of them had ever known. Christine was equally beloved. They were world citizens with an open-hearted warmth for all. They never stood on ceremony but were simply "Carl and Christine" to everyone. Christine delighted in the enthusiastic and capable way her young students took up eurythmy under her lively and vivacious direction. She and Carl did not cast judgments of "superficial" or "Ahrimanic" on the Americans they met, but saw in them instinctive Anthroposophy, generosity, and brotherhood in the will forces vibrantly inherent in America. The Americans responded to this grace-filled seeing with gratitude and admiration. Many felt guided as though by wise parents.

Not that Carl was all benevolence. He could chastise and correct. It was a bit like being straightened up by Father God! He was clear, direct, and unsentimental, yet he maintained a fervent faith in the resurrection powers of this land and this people to achieve a tranformed spiritual America—if only each individual would wake up and will it.

Carl willed it. His lectures and sermons were intense and moving. He always challenged everyone to greater participation in these serious times. His delivery began slowly, quietly, and deliberately, then a midpoint would errupt with a crescendo of powerful fire and spirit-filled will that at once riveted the listeners and lifted them to new thoughts and empowered resolves. For some it had more apocalyptic intensity than they wanted to face; others knew they were hearing one speaking as did prophets of old.

Carl was named Oberlenker for the Christian Community in 1966 and served in that capacity for America and the West from 1970 to 1985. Oberlenkers carry worldwide spiritual responsibility for the movement. Carl celebrated his last Act of Consecration service in Sacramento, California at the age of 85 in 1982. It was a profound privilege to experience this Communion service through Carl, who had been present with Rudolf Steiner for the first one.

In 1975 Carl began to give lectures in Sacramento, making the long drives from Oakland for weekly study group sessions. He always interjected phrases such as "We must prepare. . . . We have a task. . . . We must read the signs of the times. . . . Can we form a center? What can such a small group of people do? . . . Remember spiritual laws are different from earthly laws!"

Carl's repeated challenges bore fruit on a fateful night, February 22, 1976, when he announced that he and Christine would move to Sacramento, "if a group of people would come together to form a center for Anthroposophy and the future and America and mankind." (That day was the anniversary of George Washington's birth in the bi-centennial year of America, as well the 100th anniversary of Ita Wegman's birth.)

A lifetime of work had led to that moment as Carl and Christine became the catalysts for the founding of an active center for Anthroposophy and the spiritual America. What happened next was a unique and powerful spiritual experience for all of us privileged to be there. A whirlwind flame of light and enthusiasm swept the room with such uniting intensity one could only feel it was the blessing of great spiritual powers. The response was immediate. Filled with fire and hope, Rudolf Steiner College was born (first called the Sacramento Center for Anthroposophical Studies). The founding group met in an old factory building on property near the Sacramento Waldorf School. Christine gave a $5000 donation to begin the work. From those humble beginnings has arisen one of the most active anthroposophical centers in America.

Throughout 21 years it has served thousands of individuals from all over the world. During all these years, inspired by Carl, we have given continuing classes at Rudolf Steiner College about the spiritual destiny of America, to educate and awaken individuals to this country's mission. It has been a work unique to this institution.

As Rudolf Steiner College developed into an important cosmopolitan teacher training center out of the great need for Waldorf education for the coming generations, Carl and Christine continued to work with the students, and also pioneered another research group, The Ralph Waldo Emerson Study Center. Then, after 15 years of invaluable and inspiring contributions, they returned to Germany for health care needs and to take all they had experienced in America back to Europe as an awakening call for the millenium. Carl often said in serious jest, he hoped he might reincarnate rather soon and he hoped it would be in America. Always a man of action with thoughts to the future!

With Christine at his side, Carl strengthened and touched countless lives, deeply and irrevocably. Christine died in 1990. After her death, Carl spoke of the "conversations of the heart" they continued to share each day. Carl crossed in great peace, February 16, 1996, a month before his ninety-ninth birthday. I can offer no greater tribute than this. It is the spiritual insight given us through Carl's leadership that can give us the perspective and hope to face the end of the century and truly take up the work of America's destiny. May many hear the call!

Nancy Jewel Poer
Rudolf Steiner College, 1997

Epilogue

by Carl Stegmann

In a lecture around the end of 1918 (*The Mission of Michael*, December 14, 1918), Rudolf Steiner said:

> If our universities continue teaching the way they do now for three more decades, and if people continue thinking about social questions the way they do now for another thirty years, you will have a devastated Europe in thirty years.[1]

When we add thirty years to 1919, we arrive at the year 1949, the time immediately after the Second World War. Rudolf Steiner had been dead for more than two decades. What did Europe look like in those years? Millions of people suffered terribly from the aftermath of the worst war that Europe ever experienced. We did indeed behold a "devastated Europe!" We therefore have to take Rudolf Steiner's above remark most seriously.

Now, what is the part that institutions of higher learning play in this connection? All universities had—and still have today—one thing in common: Almost without exception, they are saturated with today's materialistic science. They teach the students a materialistic conception of the world, the human being, nature, and society. Those who are students today will later on become leaders of society. Many become instructors and teach materialistic thinking again to children and young people. Everyone is influenced by this and begins to think and act in the direction that is being taught by universities. Rudolf Steiner by no means failed to recognize the

267

significance of modern-day science. But he wanted to enable scientific thinking to learn to acknowledge fully the invisible, the spiritual. Thinking itself would thus have to be transformed. After decades, this new, spiritually extended thinking will then produce a transformed outer world with new social conditions—unfolding as a threefold social organism. This is just as certain as the fact that materialistic thinking produced the terrible consequences of our age. Here, we arrive at an insight of monumental significance that can be summarized in a simple sentence:

Change your thinking,
and the world will change.

In the future, a fruitful understanding between Central Europe, America, and the Orient can result only through this changed thinking, motivated by a new spirituality in schools and universities. On the occasion of the East-West Congress in Vienna, Rudolf Steiner spoke of the building of bridges to the Orient, a process that is linked to the cooperation of Central European and American spirituality.

Only when, based on principles such as those I have now described, out of the European and American spirit together, people will produce something spiritual in the general world view, only then will the bridge across to the Orient be built. (GA 83, lecture of June 10, 1922.)

ANNOTATIONS

FOR THE ENGLISH LANGUAGE EDITION

Quotations from Rudolf Steiner have been given with reference to his complete works published in German in Dornach, Switzerland by the Verlag am Goetheanum. For the benefit of readers who do not have access to that edition, the following is a list of Steiner books and lectures in English translation to which Carl Stegmann often referred in his various writings:

Archangel Michael, The (New York: Anthroposophic Press, 1994)

Awakening to Community (New York: Anthroposophic Press, 1974)

Challenge of the Times, The (New York: Anthroposophic Press, 1941)

East in the Light of the West, The (New York: Anthroposophic Press, 1940); also published in combination with Edouard Schuré's *Children of Lucifer* (Blauvelt, New York: Spiritual Science Library, a division of Garber Communications, Inc., 1986)

Fall of the Spirits of Darkness, The (London: Rudolf Steiner Press, 1993)

Four Mystery Dramas (Canada: Rudolf Steiner Centre, 1973)

From Jesus to Christ (London: Rudolf Steiner Press, 1991)

Intuitive Thinking as a Spiritual Path (New York: Anthroposophic Press, 1996); translations also published under the titles *Philosophy of Freedom* and *Philosophy of Spiritual Activity*.

Towards Social Renewal (London: Rudolf Steiner Press, 1992)

True Nature of the Second Coming, The (London: Rudolf Steiner Press, 1971)

Quotations from Emerson conform to the wording in *The Complete Writings of Ralph Waldo Emerson* (New York: Wm. H. Wise & Co., 1929).

Quotations from *The Greening of America* by Charles Reich conform to the original work in English. All other citations from German or English sources have been rendered into English by the present translator from Stegmann's German text with some help from his earlier writing on the subject given originally in English.

For Parts I and II

1   Steiner, GA 23

2   Steiner, GA 83

3   The following quotes are from Charles A. Reich, *The Greening of America*, (New York: Random House, 1970); Peter Marshall, *The American Dream*, (New York: Wm. E. Rudge's Sons, 1953); Ferdinand von Cles, *Licht aus dem Westen*, (Cologne: Thomas Wolfe and John Collier, 1957); Russell W. Davenport, *The Dignity of Man*, (New York: Harper, 1955).

4   Steiner, GA 83, lecture of June 10, 1922.

5   Steiner, GA 181, lecture of July 9, 1918.

6   Steiner, *Four Mystery Dramas*, "The Soul's Awakening," third scene.

7   Steinbeck, *The Red Pony*, (New York: Covici-Sriede, 1937).

8   Willem Zeylmans van Emmichoven, *Amerika und der Amerikanismus*, (Freiburg, 1954).

9   Ibid.

10   Walter Bühler, *Der Leib als Instrument der Seele*, Stuttgart, 1955. Translated as *Living With Your Body,* (London: Rudolf Steiner Press, 1979).

11   Steiner, GA 231, lecture of November 17, 1923.

12   Steiner, GA 206, lecture of August 14, 1921.

13   Steiner, GA 194, lecture of December 14, 1919.

14   Gabriel Marcel, *Die Erniedrigung des Menschen*, (Frankfurt, 1957).

15   Steiner, GA 186, lecture of December 6, 1918.

16   Ibid.

17   Steiner, GA 194, lecture of December 14, 1919.

18   Steiner, GA 206, lecture of August 6, 1921.

19   Steiner, GA 186, lectures of December 6 and 8, 1918.

20   Louis Bromfield, *Mr. Smith,* (New York: Harper, 1951).

21   Charles Reich, *The Greening of America*, pp. 304, 129, 225, 88, 89.

22   Ralph Waldo Emerson, *Essays*, (Cambridge, 1903).

23   Walt Whitman, "Song of Myself," (New York, 1964).

24   Steiner, GA 130, lecture of October 1, 1911.

25   Steiner, GA 107, lecture of January 1, 1909.

26   Steiner, *Philosophy of Spiritual Activity*.

27 Steiner, GA 129, lecture of August 21, 1911.

28 Steiner, GA 105, lecture of August 4, 1908.

29 Steiner, GA 40, "Michael Imagination."

30 Steiner, GA 129, lecture of August 21, 1911.

31 Steiner, GA 177, lecture of October 26, 1917.

32 Steiner, GA 171, lecture of September 24, 1916.

33 Steiner, GA 177, lecture of October 28, 1917.

34 Ralph Waldo Emerson, *Essays*.

35 Herman Melville, *Moby Dick*, (New York, 1971).

36 Diether Lauenstein, *Das Geheimnis des Wals*, (Stuttgart, 1973).

37 Steiner, GA 129, lecture of August 21, 1911.

38 Steiner, GA 182, lecture of October 9, 1918.

39 Steiner, *Anthroposophical Leading Thoughts*, (London: Rudolf Steiner Press, 1973), Letter to Members on October 12, 1924.

40 Steiner, GA 182, lecture of October 9, 1918.

41 Ibid.

42 Steiner, GA 186, lecture of December 1, 1918

43 Ibid.

44 Ibid.

45 Steiner, GA 230, lecture of October 20, 1923.

46 Steiner, GA 171, lecture of September 18, 1916.

47 William H. Prescott, *The World of the Aztecs*, (London: Gifford, 1970)

48 Ignatius Donnelly, *Atlantis: The Antediluvian World*, (New York: Harper, 1949).

49 Steiner, GA 171, lecture of September 18, 1916.

50 Ibid.

51   Ibid.

52   Ibid., lecture of September 24, 1916.

53   Ibid., lecture of September 18, 1916.

54   Ibid.

55   Ibid.

56   Revelation of John, 19:20.

57   Steiner, GA 107, lecture of January 1, 1909.

58   Steiner, GA 171, lecture of September 24, 1916.

59   Ibid.

60   Ibid., lecture of September 17, 1916.

61   Ibid.

62   Ibid.

63   Ibid.

64   Steiner, GA 107, lecture of March 22, 1909.

65   Steiner, GA 193, lecture of November 4, 1919.

66   Steiner, GA 230, lecture of October 20, 1923.

67   Steiner, GA 172, lecture of November 12, 1916.

68   Ibid.

69   Ibid.

70   Ibid.

71   Ibid.

72   Ibid.

73   Ibid.

74   Ibid.

75   Ibid.

76   Steiner, GA 186, lecture of December 1, 1918.

77   Vladimir Soloviev, "Die Rechtfertigung des Guten," in *Werke*, (Jena, 1914 ff).

78   Steiner, GA 178, lecture of November 16, 1917.

79   Werner-Christian Simonis, *Der Doppelgänger des Menschen*, (Freiburg, 1973).

80   Steiner, GA 178, lecture of November 16, 1917.

81   Steiner, GA 200, lecture of October 22, 1920.

82   George Victor Bishop, *Witness to Evil,* (Los Angeles: Nash Publishers, 1972).

83   Steiner, GA 178. lecture of November 16, 1917.

84   Ibid., lecture of November 15, 1917.

85   Ibid., lecture of November 16, 1917.

86   Ibid.

87   Ibid.

88   Steiner, *Anthroposophical Leading Thoughts*, Letter to Members on October 12, 1924.

89   Steiner, GA 178, lecture of November 16, 1917.

90   Steiner, GA 220, lecture of January 28, 1923.

91   Berthold Wulf, *Geheimnisvolle Erde,* (Schaffhausen, 1961).

92   Steiner, GA 178, lecture of November 16, 1917.

93   Ferdinand Cles, *Licht aus dem Westen,* see 3.

94   Steiner, GA 178, lecture of November 16, 1917.

95   Ibid.

96   Karl Buchleitner, "Spirituelle Medizin und der Doppelgänger" in *Mitteilungen aus der Anthroposophischen Arbeit in Deutschland,* (Stuttgart, 1973), No. 106.

97   Simonis, see 79.

98   William Peter Blatty, *The Exorcist,* (New York: Harper & Row, 1971).

99   Steiner, GA 186, lecture of lecture of December 1, 1918.

100 Ibid.

101 Steiner, GA 152, lecture of May 2, 1913.

102 Ibid.

103 Ibid.

104 Steiner, GA 118, lecture of January 25, 1910.

105 Steiner, GA 162, lecture of July 31, 1915.

106 Steiner, GA 152, lecture of May 2, 1913.

107 Ibid.

108 Steiner, GA 118, lecture of January 25, 1910.

109 Ibid.

110 Ibid., lecture of March 6, 1910.

111 Steiner, GA 130, lecture of November 4, 1911.

112 Steiner, GA.118, lecture of March 6,1910.

113 Steiner, GA 118, lecture of January 25, 1910.

114 Ibid.

115 Steiner, GA 112, lecture of July 5, 1909.

116 Steiner, GA 102, lecture of June 4, 1908.

117 Steiner, GA 112, lecture of July 5, 1909.

118 Steiner, GA 118, lecture of March 6, 1910.

119 Ibid.

120 Steiner, GA 152, lecture of May 2, 1913.

121 Astrid C. Schmitt, "A Comparison of Some Philosophical Views of W.B. Yeats and Rudolf Steiner with Emphasis on the Second Coming," unpublished M.A. thesis, California State University, Sacramento, 1975.

122 Steiner, GA 200, lecture of October 31, 1920.

123 Ibid.

124 Ibid.

125 Steiner, GA 193, lecture of November 4, 1919.

126 Ibid.

127 Ibid.

128 Ibid.

129 Ibid.

130 Steiner, GA 107, lecture of January 1, 1909.

131 Steiner, GA 191, lecture of November 15, 1919.

132 Steiner, GA 182, lecture of October 9, 1918.

133 Ibid.

134 Steiner, GA 193, lecture of November 4, 1919.

135 Steiner, GA 193, lecture of October 27, 1919.

136 Steiner, GA 191, lecture of November 2, 1919.

137 Steiner, GA 193, lecture of October 27, 1919.

138 Steiner, GA 191, lecture of November 1, 1919.

139 Ibid.

140 Ibid.

141 Steiner, GA 193, lecture of November 4, 1919. Also see Hans-Werner Schroeder, "The End of the Century and Ahriman's Incarnation in the Following Millennium" and "The Incarnation of Ahriman and the Asuras,"and "Sorath and the End of the Century" in: Mitteilungen aus der Anthropo. Arbeit in Deutschland. Stuttgart 1978/1979, #125, 126, 127. In these articles, the differentiation between Ahriman and the Sorath-being is depicted. The Sorath-being is designated with the occult number 666 and pointedly makes use of the 666-year rhythm.

142 Steiner, GA 182, lecture of October 16, 1918.

143 Steiner, GA 171, lecture of September 25, 1916.

144 Steiner, GA 206, lecture of August 6, 1921.

145 Steiner, GA 102, lecture of April 20, 1908.

146 Ibid.

147 Ibid.

148 Steiner, GA 194, lecture of November 23, 1919.

149 Steiner, GA 240, lecture of July 20, 1924.

150 Ibid.

151 Ibid.

152 Ibid.

153 Ibid.

154 Steiner, GA 174, lecture of January 21, 1917.

155 Steiner, GA 107, lecture of January 1, 1909.

156 Steiner, GA 174, lecture of January 22, 1917.

157 Ibid.

158 Ibid.

159 Ibid.

160 Ibid.

161 Ibid.

162 Ibid.

163 Ibid.

164 Steiner, GA 177, lecture of October 14, 1917.

165 Steiner, GA 191, lecture of November 15, 1919.

166 Ibid.

167 Ibid.

168 Steiner, GA 162, lecture of August 1, 1915.

169 Steiner, GA 191, lecture of November 15, 1919

170 Ibid.

171 Steiner, GA 178, lecture of November 16, 1917.

172 Ibid.

173 Steiner, GA 219, lecture of December 3, 1922.

174   Ibid.

175   Ibid.

176   Ibid.

177   Steiner, GA 26, chapter 9.

178   Steiner, GA 174, lecture of January 20, 1917.

179   Steiner, GA 205, lecture of July 3, 1921.

180   Steiner, GA 193, lecture of November 4, 1919.

181   Steiner, GA 177, lecture of October 20, 1917.

182   Steiner, GA 104, lecture of June 25, 1908. See also Emil Bock, *The Apocalypse of St. John*, (London: Christian Community Press, 1957).

183   Steiner, GA 240, lecture of July 20, 1924.

184   Rev. 9.

185   Rev. 10:5f.

186   Rev. 11:19.

187   1 Cor. 15:51.

188   Steiner, GA 194, lecture of December 14, 1919.

189   Steiner, GA 349, lecture of March 3, 1924.

190   Ibid.

191   Ibid.

192   Ibid.

193   Steiner, GA 10, *Knowledge of the Higher Worlds and Its Attainment*, 'Control of Thoughts and Feelings.'

194   Steiner, GA 132, lecture of November 14, 1911.

195   Steiner, GA 193, lecture of February 11, 1919.

196   Lauenstein, see 36.

197   Steiner, GA 206, lecture of August 20, 1921.

198   Steiner, *Anthroposophical Leading Thoughts* "From Nature to Sub-Nature."

199 Steiner, GA 118, lecture of January 25, 1910.

200 Ibid.

201 Ibid.

202 Steiner, GA 200, lecture of October 22, 1920.

203 John 3.

204 Steiner, GA 200, lecture of October 22, 1920.

205 Steiner, GA 194, lecture of December 14, 1919.

206 Steiner, GA 349, lecture of March 3, 1924.

FOR PART III

1   Ralph Waldo Emerson, *Representative Men*, "Goethe."

2   Emerson, *Essays*, "Intellect."

3   Steiner, GA 1.

4   Steiner, GA 2.

5   Steiner, GA 157, lecture of June 22, 1915.

6   Ibid.

7   Emerson, *Representative Men*, "Shakespeare."

8   Ibid. "Goethe."

9   See 5.

10   Steiner, GA 178, lecture of November 16, 1917.

11   Brooks Atkinson,*The Selected Writings of Ralph Waldo Emerson*, (New York: The Modern Library,1940).

12   Stephen E. Whicher, *Selections from Ralph Waldo Emerson,* (Boston: Houghton Mifflin, 1957).

13   Emerson, *Essays*, "The Over-Soul."

14   Ibid.

15   Ibid.

16   Emerson, *Essays,* "Nature."

17 Acts 17:27f. Translated from E. Bock's German translation of New Testament.

18 Emerson, *Conduct of Life,* "Worship."

19 Emerson, *Essays,* "Self-Reliance."

20 *Ralph Waldo Emerson. Ein Weiser Amerikas spricht zu uns,* excerpts from his works compiled by Helene Siegfried, Hamburg 1954.

21 Edgar Lee Masters, *The Living Thoughts of Emerson* (London, 1941).

22 Emerson, "The American Scholar."

23 Emerson, *Conduct of Life,* "Considerations by the Way."

24 Ibid.

25 Emerson, *Conduct of Life,* "Worship."

26 See 12, p. 144.

27 See 21, p. 17f.

28 Emerson, *Essays,* "Nature."

29 Emerson, *Poems,* "Brahma.""

30 Emerson, "The Transcendentalist."

31 Emerson, *Essays,* "Intellect."

32 Emerson, *Conduct of Life,* "Worship."

33 Emerson, *Essays,* "Love."

34 Emerson, "Man the Reformer."

35 Emerson, "The American Scholar."

36 Emerson, "The Young American."

37 Emerson, *Conduct of Life,* "Fate."

38 Emerson, *Essays,* "The Poet."

39 Steiner, GA 21.

40 Emerson, *Essays,* ""The Over-Soul."

41 Emerson, *Representative Men,* "Uses of Great Men."